Junior History

Book 2

GALORE PARK

Junior History
Book 2

Michael Webb

Series Editor: Niall Murphy

www.galorepark.co.uk

Published by Galore Park Publishing Ltd,
338 Euston Road, London, NW1 3BH
www.galorepark.co.uk

Text copyright © Michael Webb 2007
Illustrations copyright © Galore Park 2007

The right of Michael Webb to be identified as the author of this Work has been asserted by him in accordance with sections 77 and 78 of the Copyright, Designs and Patents Act 1988.

Design and typography The Design Gallery, Suffolk
Illustrations by Gwyneth Williamson, Rosie Brooks and Jane Humphrey
Printed in Dubai

ISBN: 978 1 902984 95 7

First published 2007, reprinted 2010, 2012, 2014

A set of answers to accompany this course is available to teachers from www.galorepark.co.uk

Details of other Galore Park publications are available at www.galorepark.co.uk

ISEB Revision Guides, publications and examination papers may also be obtained from Galore Park.

Acknowledgements

I would like to thank my sister, Rosie Lakin, and Stephen Sides, Headmaster of Northbourne Park School near Deal in Kent, for their help and encouragement.

Contents

Chapter 4 Life in 5ᵗʰ century BC Athens

Chapter 5 Macedonia and Alexander the Great

Chapter 6 Who were the Romans?

Chapter 7 Life in the Republic

Chapter 8 Rome's domination of Italy

Chapter 9 Civil war

Chapter 10 Roman entertainment

Introduction

In the past, when classical languages were a compulsory part of the timetable, learning Latin (and Greek) was regarded purely as an exercise in language and was rejected by many pupils as a boring subject, to be dropped at the earliest opportunity. Today classics teachers have to compete with many other subjects and must capture the imaginations of their students. In my own school children could choose between Latin and Spanish and I am sure that most of those who chose Latin were attracted by classical background studies, especially mythology and history. Who can fail to be excited by the battles of Thermopylae and Marathon, the exploits of Alexander the Great, the life and death of Julius Caesar? For those who are unfortunate enough not to learn Latin, the study of Greek and Roman history is a pleasure to be savoured.

Michael Webb

2007

ANCIENT GREECE

MEANWHILE OVER IN ROME

In the beginning was... a blind poet.

HOMER
8TH CENTURY BC

800BC

Romulus and Remus were building a new city.

THE FOUNDATION OF ROME 753 BC

700BC

The Greeks loved his stories. But then the Persians came...

600BC

Soon the Romans grew tired of kings...

THE PERSIAN WARS 490-480 BC

500BC

EXPULSION OF TARQUINIUS THE PROUD 509 BC

Once they'd beaten the Persians, the Greeks began fighting each other...

THE PELOPONNESIAN WARS 431-404 BC

Rome flourished as a republic, but life was not always easy...

After years of fighting, a new hero appeared...

400BC

ROME CAPTURED BY GAULS 387 BC

ALEXANDER THE GREAT 336-323 BC

300BC

And the Carthaginians just kept coming back for more...

THE PUNIC WARS 264-202 BC

200BC

But his empire broke up on his death – and that was the end of that!

100BC

Once the Romans had polished off Carthage, there was no looking back...

Although, some Romans were easily distracted...

JULIUS CAESAR CONQUERS GAUL

50BC

ANTONY FALLS FOR CLEOPATRA 42 BC

AUGUSTUS BECOMES THE 1ST ROMAN EMPEROR 27 BC

After defeating Antony at the Battle of Actium, Octavian became sole ruler...

0AD

CLAUDIUS INVADES BRITAIN 43 AD

50AD

The Roman Empire continued to expand...

THE ROMAN EMPIRE UNDER TRAJAN 116 AD

And reached its height under Trajan.

But it wasn't to last...

300AD

CONSTANTINE MOVES HIS CAPITAL TO BYZANTIUM 330 AD

THE FALL OF THE ROMAN EMPIRE 476 AD

And after years of decline and fall...

500AD

It fell!

Chapter 1
Who were the Greeks?

You probably know about the Ancient Greeks, who sailed with Agamemnon to Troy and fought the Trojans for ten long years. You may also know of the Ancient Greeks who invented the Olympic Games, who invented drama, who wrote the first History. You probably know some stories from Greece – Greek myths – and you may have visited ancient temples in Greece. But let's stand back now and ask ourselves, who were these Ancient Greeks, and why do we still learn about them today?

The city states

Greece was not one country, as it is today, but a number of separate city states, each with its own government, linked only by their common language. **Agamemnon** and the other Greeks who attacked **Troy** were called **Achaeans**. After the Trojan war the Achaeans returned to Greece but soon invaders from the north called **Dorians** drove them from the **Peloponnese**, the southern part of Greece. Some Achaeans left Greece and settled in Asia Minor, others remained in **Attica**, the region around Athens. Both the Achaeans and the Dorians spoke Greek but in different ways. They called themselves **Hellenes**, and people who didn't speak Greek they referred to as *barbaroi* from which the English word 'barbarian' is derived.

Greek religion

The Hellenes, or Greeks, believed in many gods, some great and worshipped by everyone, others minor gods, known only by the inhabitants of a particular place. They believed that **nymphs** (female spirits) lived in each tree, river or mountain.

In the countryside lived **Pan**, a goat-like creature who frightened lonely travellers (and gave us the word panic). But most important of all were the gods and goddesses who were thought to live on **Mount Olympus**, the highest mountain in Greece. Their king was **Zeus**. His brother, **Poseidon**, was god of the sea, and another brother, **Hades**, ruled the gloomy kingdom under the earth where the souls of the dead went.

The gods of Olympus

The Greeks didn't think that their gods were good and fair and perfect. Gods had all the good and bad points that humans had but magnified a hundred times. Zeus often lost his temper and hurled thunderbolts at anyone who upset him. His wife **Hera** could be cruel and jealous. Once, when Zeus was chasing a girl called **Leda**, Hera changed her into a swan. Zeus, quick as a flash, changed himself into a swan too. Later, Leda laid an egg and, when it hatched, out came two boys and two girls. The boys we know as *Gemini*, the Twins, one of the signs of the Zodiac. The girls were **Helen**, later famous as Helen of Troy, and **Clytemnestra** who became the wife of Agamemnon, leader of the expedition to Troy.

The names of the best known gods are listed here.

The gods and godesses of Greece

Greek Name	Description
Zeus	ruler of the gods
Hera	queen of the gods
Poseidon	god of the sea
Hades	god of the underworld
Athene	goddess of wisdom and the arts
Artemis	goddess of hunting and the moon
Apollo	god of music, archery and the sun
Aphrodite	goddess of love and beauty
Ares	god of war
Dionysus	god of wine
Hephaestus	god of fire and metalwork
Demeter	goddess of the harvest
Hermes	messenger of the gods

Myths

Hades and Persephone in the Underworld

A myth is a story which was told to explain things which people at the time would not have understood. For example, why do we have summer and winter? The Greeks believed that there had been a Golden Age when the weather had always been warm and sunny and fruit and cereals grew all the year round. **Demeter**, the goddess of plants and trees, had a daughter, **Persephone**, who was kidnapped while she was playing with her friends.

Hades, the god of the underworld, had no wife to share his dark kingdom, so had decided to seize Persephone and make her his queen. Nobody knew where Persephone was and her heartbroken mother stopped causing the corn to grow and the trees to produce their fruit for mankind. When Zeus discovered what had happened, he decided that Persephone should spend six months of the year with her mother, a time when plants and crops would grow, and six months with Hades in the underworld, when nothing would grow.

Legends

Legends are stories about heroes. Greek heroes were larger-than-life human beings whose father or mother was one of the gods. **Heracles** (or Hercules as the Romans called him) was the son of Zeus and Alcmene. Because Hera was angry at Zeus's behaviour, she hated Heracles. As a baby he was too big for his cot and slept in a shield. One night Hera sent two powerful snakes to kill him. Heracles woke up and strangled them. Later, when he was married with children, Hera sent him mad. In his madness Heracles killed his own children. To make up for this horrible deed he was forced to carry out twelve labours. One of these was to clean out the stables of **Augeias**.

Augeias had herds of magnificent cattle whose dung had been allowed to pile up over the years so that it was many metres deep. Heracles solved the problem by changing the course of two rivers so that the water flowed through the cowsheds and instantly swept all the filth away.

Oracles: the story of Perseus

The Greeks believed that it was possible to discover what would happen in the future by going to an *oracle*. The oracle was a place sacred to a god, normally **Apollo** who was the god of prophecy, the art of telling the future. The most famous and the most ancient was at **Delphi**, a place to the north of Athens, where the **Pythia**, the priestess of Apollo, told the future in exchange for gold.

Acrisius, the king of Argos, was worried because he had no sons to take his place when he died. He went to Delphi to see the Pythia. She told him his daughter **Danae** would have a son but that this boy, his grandson, would kill him. Immediately Acrisius locked Danae up in a room made of bronze. However, one day Zeus came to her in a shower of gold and she had a baby.

She called him **Perseus**. When Acrisius found out, he had mother and son put in a wooden chest which was thrown into the sea. The chest was washed up on an island and found by **Dictys**, the brother of the island's king, **Polydectes**. Dictys took them home and looked after them.

When Perseus had grown into a brave young man, Polydectes wanted to marry Danae. He tricked Perseus into boasting that he would bring back the head of the Gorgon **Medusa**. Medusa was a monster with snakes for hair who could turn into stone

anyone who gazed on her. The gods helped Perseus with gifts of a polished shield, winged sandals and a helmet of invisibility. He looked at Medusa's reflection in his shield and struck off her head. He carried the head in a bag and used it as a weapon against his enemies who were turned to stone, or 'petrified'.

Later, when Perseus was travelling home to visit his grandfather, he took part in an athletics contest. He threw the discus further than anyone else. The discus was caught by the wind and killed a man in the crowd. It was, of course, his grandfather Acrisius. The oracle's prophecy had come true.

How do we know?

How do we know that the Greeks believed in the gods on Mount Olympus and in the stories about heroes and monsters? As historians, we need to look at the evidence. The writings of the poets **Homer** and **Hesiod** are full of ideas about how the world was made and how the gods came into being.

For example, Homer, in his poem the *Iliad*, wrote: 'Now after twelve days, the gods came back to Olympus, and Zeus led the way.'

Much later, **Pindar**, a poet of the 5th century BC, told how Zeus spoke to one of his sons, offering that he would live forever: 'If you would escape from death and dwell on Olympus with me, this may be yours.'

In plays by great writers like **Aeschylus** and **Sophocles**, the gods often take part in the stories and it is clear that the audience was familiar with them. We can also look at the pottery in everyday use which was decorated with pictures of gods and heroes.

These are just a few examples of literally thousands of references to the gods in the writings and artefacts of Ancient Greece that have survived.

. . . .

Exercise 1.1

1. Which Greek city lies in the region called Attica?

2. What is the name of the highest mountain in Greece?

3. Gemini (twins) is one of the signs of the zodiac. Try to name at least three more signs and say what they mean.

4. Who was the mother of Heracles?

5. Athens takes its name from one of the goddesses of Mount Olympus. Which one?

6. What was the name of Persephone's mother?

7. What were the invaders called who drove the Achaeans from the Peloponnese?

8. What did Heracles use as a cot?

Exercise 1.2

Complete the following sentences:

1. _____ were female spirits who lived in trees, rivers and mountains.

2. The god of the sea was _____.

3. Clytemnestra became the wife of _____.

4. Hades captured _____, the daughter of Demeter.

5. _____ drove Heracles mad.

6. The most ancient oracle was at _____.

Exercise 1.3

Explain what is meant by the following:

1. to petrify

2. an oracle

3. *barbaroi*

4. the Pythia

5. a prophecy

Exercise 1.4

Most Greek writers, like Homer and Pindar, wrote about the Greek gods with great respect. A playwright called **Aristophanes**, however, has the god **Dionysus** as a character in his play *The Frogs*. In the play, Heracles comes onto the stage and makes fun of Dionysus, causing the audience to laugh at the god! Write a short play or story of your own involving one or more of the gods of Mount Olympus. Read or perform this to your class.

Exercise 1.5

You may have to do some research, perhaps on the internet or in the library, to answer some of these questions.

1. Imagine that you are Perseus. Tell your story from as early as you can remember.

2. You are Heracles telling the story of your life. Give an account of your adventures as you performed your Twelve Labours.

3. Tell the story of the kidnap of Persephone from her point of view.

4. When Theseus was a young man he had to make a dangerous journey to Athens. Find out about this and write a brief description of his adventures.

5. Tell the story of any other legendary hero you have learnt about.

Chapter 2
The wars with Persia

The Persian empire

We read in the Bible, in the Book of Daniel, about Nebuchadnezzar. He was the King of **Babylon** and ruled the Babylonian Empire from 605 to 562 BC. A thousand miles away to the west was **Lydia**, the kingdom of Croesus who was so very wealthy that today we say of a multi-millionaire that he is 'as rich as Croesus'. Between these two great empires lived the **Medes** and the **Persians** and, when these two great nations joined together, their king **Cyrus the Great** decided to go to war against his two great neighbours. Cyrus proved victorious and Babylon and Lydia became part of the **Persian empire**, the greatest empire there had ever been. After the death of Cyrus and his son who followed him, there came a king called **Darius**, whose empire stretched from the borders of India in the east to Lydia in the west and included cities in Ionia which had earlier been built by the Greeks.

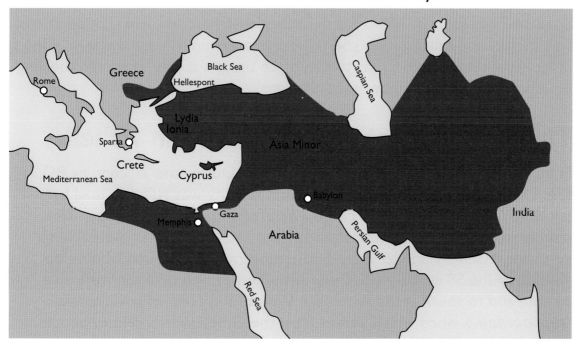

The Persian empire in the 5th century BC

Greek colonies

The cities in Greece expanded during the 7th and 6th centuries BC and their populations grew. Young and daring people left home to settle in other lands around the Mediterranean. They kept in touch with their mother cities, speaking Greek and keeping the same customs and way of life as their parents. Those who had settled in Ionia were used to ruling themselves and disliked the rulers forced on them by the Persians. In 499 BC they rebelled, drove out their Persian rulers and then asked Athens for help. Athens sent twenty ships and, together with the Ionians, attacked and set fire to **Sardis**, the Persian capital in the west. When word reached Darius he was furious. 'Who are the Athenians?' he cried. He shot an arrow into the sky and called on his god to help him to punish the Athenians. One of his servants was told to say to him three times a day as he served the king his dinner, 'Master, remember the Athenians'.

The development of democracy in Athens

In its early history Athens was ruled by kings. During the 7th century BC, these kings began to lose their power and the city was ruled instead by a few noble families, a system called *oligarchy*: the rule of the few. The people were divided into classes and all but the lowest class were able to go to the Assembly and to vote. This arrangement continued to develop so that, by the 5th century BC, free men, whether rich or poor, were able to vote and to speak in the Assembly. We call this form of government *democracy*, a word which comes from the Greek words *demos,* 'people' and *kratos,* 'power': the rule of the people for the people. Once the Greeks had experienced democracy they never wanted to go back to being ruled by kings, and that is why they were prepared to fight against the Persians, however one-sided the war would be.

The first Persian invasion

The Persians punished the Ionians severely for their rebellion. The Athenians were very upset, both because they couldn't do anything to help their fellow Greeks and because they knew that they were next. In 492 BC Darius sent an invasion force to Greece but the fleet was hit by a storm which destroyed two hundred ships. In 490 BC another great Persian army arrived in Greece, and Darius sent messengers to all the Greek cities and islands to demand their surrender. Athens, Sparta and many others refused. This meant war. The Persian fleet anchored off **Marathon** on the east coast of Attica about twenty miles north of Athens.

The Battle of Marathon, 490 BC

The Athenians were in great danger. They sent a swift runner called **Pheidippides** to Sparta to ask for help. The Spartans were celebrating a religious festival at the time and said that they couldn't set off before the next full moon. Pheidippides ran back to tell the Athenians and then, exhausted by his running, died on the spot.

Miltiades, one of the Athenian generals, suggested the army should go to Marathon to fight the Persians. Some objected that this would leave Athens undefended, but Miltiades had his way and, a day later, nine thousand Athenians were looking down from the hills near Marathon on the great Persian fleet. Miltiades daringly suggested attacking the Persians immediately and again he won the argument. The generals drew up a line of battle the same length as the Persian line but with most of the soldiers on the wings, leaving the centre very weak. The Athenians advanced quickly down the hill and, when the two lines crashed together, the Persians burst

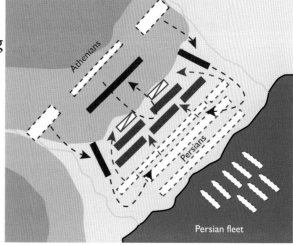

Persian fleet

The Battle of Marathon

through the centre but were forced back on the left and on the right. Then, as planned, the Greek wings turned and attacked the Persian centre from behind. Those Persians who survived the hand-to-hand fighting fled to their ships which immediately set sail, hoping to reach Athens before the army could get back. But, as they approached the harbour at Athens, they saw the Athenian army which, even after a difficult battle, had marched swiftly back to save the city. The Persians sailed home and the Athenians found themselves celebrating a most unlikely victory. After the full moon, two thousand Spartans arrived at the battlefield, praised the Athenians for a fine victory, and went back to Sparta.

The second Persian invasion

In 486 BC Darius died and was succeeded by his son **Xerxes**, who gathered together a mighty army from all parts of the empire. It assembled at the **Hellespont**, the narrow strip of sea which separates Asia Minor from Greece. Xerxes built two bridges made of boats tied together so that the army could cross safely. During the night a storm destroyed both bridges and Xerxes was so angry that he had all the engineers who had built the bridge killed. He also ordered that the waters of the Hellespont should be whipped to punish them for resisting the great king of Persia.

The Greeks prepare for war

The Greeks were aware that the Persians would return and spent the next ten years getting ready. By now the Spartans had the strongest army in Greece, while Athens had the most powerful navy. Silver had been discovered in Attica, which made the Athenians very rich. Most people thought that each citizen should receive a share but **Themistocles**, a great politician of the time, persuaded his fellow Athenians that the money should be spent on building warships to defend their city. At a meeting of the leaders of many Greek cities and islands, it was decided that supreme command of their united army and navy should be given to **Leonidas**, one of the Spartan kings.

The Battle of Thermopylae, 480 BC

In 480 BC, ten years after the disaster at Marathon, Xerxes marched with his mighty army into Greece, conquering all who stood in his path. However, when he came to a place called **Thermopylae**, a narrow pass with mountains on one side and the sea on the other, he found that it was being defended by Leonidas with an army of a few thousand Greeks, including three hundred Spartans. The Persians attacked but were driven back time and time again. Unfortunately for Leonidas and his men, however, a Greek traitor showed the Persians a path which led through the woods and over the hills to a place where they could attack the Greeks from behind. Realising that he was beaten, Leonidas sent the bulk of his army away but remained with his faithful Spartans to defend the pass. 'When the Persians fire their arrows,' said someone, 'they blot out the sun.' 'Good news!' said another. 'That way we can fight in the shade!' Many Persians died in the battle that followed, but eventually Leonidas and all his men were killed. Later, a memorial was set up on the battlefield. It read,

'Go tell the Spartans, stranger passing by,
That here, obedient to their laws, we lie.'

The Leonidas Monument. A present day memorial to the fallen Greeks at Thermopylae

'Trust in your wooden walls'

From Thermopylae Xerxes and his army marched on to Athens. To their amazement, they found the city nearly empty. They entered the city, looting and destroying everything which lay in their path. Messages of triumph were sent back to Persia saying that Athens had been punished. But what had happened to the inhabitants of Athens? The city had sent messengers to the oracle at Delphi to find out how to defend themselves against the Persians. The oracle had replied, 'Trust in your wooden walls.' Some people had thought that the wooden walls were those round the **Acropolis**, the fortified hill in the centre of the city. Themistocles persuaded the Assembly that the wooden walls were their ships; they should abandon the city and so, while the citizens took refuge on the nearby island of **Salamis**, the army boarded the ships and waited for the Persians to arrive.

The Battle of Salamis, 480 BC

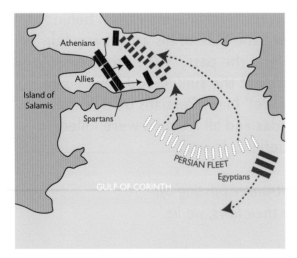

The Battle of Salamis

The Greek fleet, which was mostly made up of Athenian ships, was in the bay of **Eleusis**, between the island of Salamis and the mainland. The Spartan plan was to sail south and to defend the **Peloponnese** by blocking the narrow *isthmus*, the thin strip of land connecting the Peloponnese with the rest of Greece, so that the Persians couldn't march on Sparta. Themistocles realised that this would spell disaster for the Athenians who were now refugees on the island of Salamis, north of the isthmus. He was a very cunning man and now he sent a message to Xerxes, pretending to be his friend and warning him that the Greek fleet was about to escape. Xerxes fell for this trick and blocked the two exits from the bay. The Persian ships were big and difficult to manoeuvre and found themselves at a disadvantage once they entered the waters of the bay. The Greek ships, on the other hand, which were smaller and able to turn quickly, were soon destroying and sinking their enemy. Xerxes, sitting on a hill-top on his throne, saw two hundred of his ships destroyed and their crews all killed or drowned. Reluctantly he was forced to retreat back over the Hellespont to Persia.

How do we know?

We would know very little about the Persian wars if we didn't have the *Histories* of **Herodotus**. Herodotus was born in around 484 BC, in a city in Asia Minor. He was forced to leave his city and went on long journeys to Egypt, Sicily, Italy and the Ukraine. He returned with stories, some of them incredible, about the places he had seen and the people he had met. He also wrote down details of events which were closer to home. He called this work *historie*, a Greek word meaning 'inquiry'. Our word 'history' comes from that word. He was the first man to write what we now call history. As a result he is known as 'the Father of History'. Later historians said he was unfair in his writing but recently modern historians have said that his work is remarkably accurate, given that it was written long after the events he was describing, when most of the people who took part were dead. Unfortunately we have no Persian writings about the Persian wars, and we must always remember that the picture which Herodotus gives us is likely to be one-sided.

The Greek alphabet

Herodotus wrote his history in Greek. The Greek alphabet consists of twenty-four letters and on the next page you will find printed the capitals (which in many cases are like ours), the 'small' letters (which are rather different), and their equivalent in the letters which we use.

The Greek alphabet

Name	Capital	Small	Equivalent
alpha	A	α	a
beta	B	β	b
gamma	Γ	γ	g
delta	Δ	δ	d
epsilon	E	ε	ĕ (as in 'egg')
zeta	Z	ζ	z
eta	H	η	ē (as in 'there')
theta	Θ	θ	th
iota	I	ι	i
kappa	K	$\varkappa$	k or c
lambda	Λ	λ	l
mu	M	μ	m
nu	N	ν	n
xi	Ξ	ξ	x
omicron	O	o	ŏ (as in 'pot')
pi	Π	π	p
rho	P	ϱ	r or rh
sigma	Σ	σ/ς*	s
tau	T	τ	t
upsilon	Y	υ	u or y
phi	Φ	ϕ	ph
chi	X	χ	ch (as in 'chorus')
psi	Ψ	ψ	ps
omega	Ω	ω	ō (as in 'or')

*The Greek letter *sigma* (s) was σ, except when the letter came at the end of a word, when it was written as ς.

Note: ' written over or in front of a vowel at the beginning of a word makes the noise that the letter 'h' makes in front of a word. This sign is called a *rough breathing*. Thus, the Greek word for 'the' is ὁ (pronounced 'ho').

If a word begins with a vowel, but without the 'h' sound, a sign called a *smooth breathing* is written; it makes no sound, but is there simply to show that there is no 'h' sound. Thus the Greek word for 'name' is ὄνομα (pronounced 'onoma').

Exercise 2.1

1. Practise writing the Greek letters.

2. Write these Greek names in the letters we use:

   Ζευς   Ἀφροδιτη   Ὀδυσσευς

3. These Greek words have become English words without being changed in any way. What are they?

   κινημα   κλιμαξ   χαρακτηρ   ἠλεκτρον   ὁριζων   διαγνωσις

4. Now try writing these English words in Greek letters:

   drama   nĕctar   basis   catastrŏphē   ŏrchēstra   scēnē

5. λογος (logos) in Greek means 'word' and sometimes 'study'.

   Join the following words with λογος (logos) to form English words which are all connected with 'study' or 'science'. What do these words mean? You might need a dictionary to help you.

   e.g. γη = earth, hence 'geology' = the study of the earth.

μυθος = story	βιος = life	ψυχη = soul, mind
θεος = god	τεχνη = skill	ἀρχαιος = ancient

Exercise 2.2

1. Which king of Lydia was 'very wealthy'?

2. In which year did the Ionian Greeks rebel against the Persians?

3. What is the name of the Persian king who invaded Greece in 490 BC?

4. What is the name of the runner whom the Athenians sent to Sparta for help before the Battle of Marathon?

5. What stopped the Spartans coming at once to Marathon?

6. What is the name of the Athenian general who suggested the army should attack the Persians at Marathon?

7. Who was given overall command of the Greek forces during the second invasion of 480 BC?

8. In which year were the battles of Thermopylae and Salamis?

. . . .

Exercise 2.3

Complete the following sentences:

1. The Greeks who settled in Ionia were used to _____ government.

2. To help the Ionian Greeks the Athenians sent _____ ships.

3. The system of rule by a few noble families is called _____.

4. Marathon is on the east coast of _____.

5. In 486 BC Darius died and was succeeded by his son _____.

6. The _____ is the narrow strip of sea which separates Asia Minor from Greece.

7. _____ persuaded the Athenians to spend the profits of their silver mine on ships.

8. In 480 BC the Athenians abandoned Athens and sailed to the island of _____.

Exercise 2.4

Explain what is meant by the following:

1. oligarchy

2. the wings of a line of battle

3. a pass (Thermopylae, for example)

4. an isthmus

5. democracy

. . . .

Exercise 2.5

Herodotus tells us that Themistocles wrote secretly to Xerxes, pretending to be his friend. Later we learn that he sent another message to Xerxes, warning him that the victorious Greeks were going to break the bridge of ships across the Hellespont, cutting off the Persians' way back to Persia.

Write the letters which you imagine Themistocles sent to Xerxes. Then write the replies which you imagine he received from Xerxes.

. . . .

Exercise 2.6

1. You are a Persian soldier at the Battle of Marathon. You have been put in the middle of the line of battle and you are expecting an easy victory. Tell the story of what happened.

2. Imagine that you are an Athenian citizen sitting on a hill on the island of Salamis. Describe the scene as the Persian ships enter the bay of Eleusis and how you feel as the battle develops.

Chapter 3
Cities and civil wars

The two most powerful cities in 5th century Greece were Athens and Sparta. These two cities were as different as they could be. When they faced the same enemy, the Persians, they managed to find a way to work together, but after that, they trusted each other less and less until they were each other's worst enemy.

Sparta

The region around the city of Sparta was called **Laconia**. While Athens managed to live on friendly terms with the people of Attica, Sparta conquered Laconia and held on to it by using brute force and fear. Those who gave in to the Spartans were called *perioikoi* ('those who dwell around') and were able to live in peace, though they were never allowed to become

Spartan citizens. Those who resisted were called **Helots** and, although they were not exactly slaves, they had to do everything the Spartans said. An organisation of Spartan spies, a sort of secret police, watched over the Helots and killed any who resisted. The Spartans soon realised that they were outnumbered in their own country, so they had to be strong and always ready to fight. They avoided trade with other cities so that their citizens would not have contact with dangerous political ideas, like democracy. They banned all luxuries and lived a tough life.

At the age of seven, boys were taken from their parents and made to live together in barracks. They were taught to be soldiers and they soon learned to deal with cold, hunger and harsh discipline. They learnt to read so that they could study passages about war from Homer and other authors. From an early age they had a hard life and had to run, wrestle and throw the javelin, all to make themselves into soldiers. They owned only one item of clothing. Once a year, at a festival dedicated to Artemis, they had to steal cheeses from the altar while all the time they were being whipped. Later in their lives they were allowed to marry but they had to remain in barracks until they reached the age of thirty. Girls were taught to become the wives and mothers of tough soldiers. It is said that a Spartan mother sent her son into battle with these words: 'Return from battle either with your shield or on it!' She was referring to the fact that a soldier who ran away in battle would throw away his shield, while one who was killed would be carried back home on it. A Spartan mother would not welcome back a son who had run away from a battle.

Athens

When the Persians left after the Battle of Salamis, the Athenians returned to find their city in ruins. They started work immediately on rebuilding the temples and houses of their city. But, when they started to build the city walls, the Spartans sent messengers to tell them to stop. If they rebuilt the walls, said the Spartans, the city could be used as a fortress by the Persians if they returned. The Athenians realised that this was not the real reason;

the Spartans wanted Athens to stay weak. They therefore set every able-bodied man to work on the walls. Themistocles went to Sparta to talk about it, and his meeting with the Spartans went on so long that, by the time it ended, the walls were complete.

Unlike the Spartans, the Athenians thrived on trade. Their ships went to every part of the known world, buying and selling goods, and Athens became rich and powerful. The Athenians spent most of this money on making the city a beautiful place to live, with new temples on the Acropolis and public buildings in the **Agora**, the most important public space in the city (equivalent to the Roman Forum). Poets, artists, musicians and philosophers were attracted to the city. Changes in politics meant that every citizen could take part in running the city, though we must remember that more than half the population – women, slaves and foreigners – were not allowed to vote.

An artist's impression of the Acropolis in Athens in the 5th century

The Confederacy of Delos

You can understand that those living in the cities and islands round the Mediterranean were worried after the Persian invasions. What if the Persians returned? They felt weak and unprotected and asked Athens to join them so that they could help each other against their enemies. Athens agreed and suggested that every city or island should join what they called a

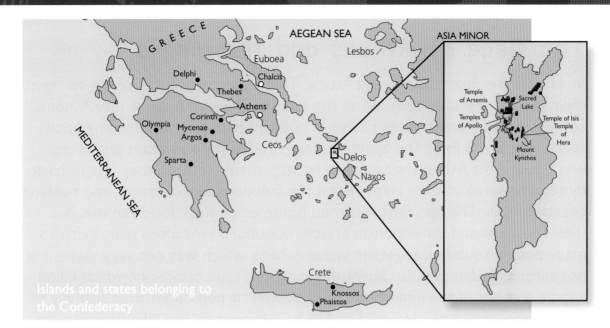

Islands and states belonging to the Confederacy

'**Confederacy**', give ships or money, and that this money should be kept on the island of **Delos**. Delos was an island sacred to Apollo, who was said to have been born there, so it was thought to be safe from thieves.

As time passed, some cities and islands found the payments more than they could afford and tried to leave the Confederacy. The Athenians reacted violently to this and used force to keep the Confederacy together. At the same time they moved the money from Delos to Athens 'where it would be safer'. **Pericles**, a great politician of the 5th century BC, used the money to rebuild the temples in Athens. He said the fleet was already big enough and there was no need to build any more. After all, he reasoned, Athens had kept her side of the bargain by keeping the rest of the Confederacy safe.

The Peloponnesian War Part 1: 431-421 BC

In this way the Confederacy of Delos became the Athenian Empire. The Spartans, who were the most powerful race in the Peloponnese, became more and more afraid of the Athenians and formed their own friendships with other cities on the mainland of Greece, in case war broke out with Athens. Then in 433 BC **Corcyra** (an island which we now call Corfu) had a disagreement with her 'mother city' **Corinth** and asked Athens for support. Corinth reported the whole matter to Sparta and war broke out. It was bound to be a long war because, while the Spartan army was the best in Greece, Athens had a much better navy.

The siege of Athens and the plague

In 431 BC the Spartans invaded Attica. There was no point in trying to resist their army, so Pericles ordered all the country people to come into Athens. Some of them found houses to live in but others had to camp in any open space they could find. The Spartans destroyed farms and crops and there was nothing the Athenians could do to stop them. Instead, they fought back by sending some of their ships round the Peloponnese, capturing and robbing coastal towns. The Spartans returned home when their food ran out, but their invasions and the Athenian attacks continued year after year. With so many people squashed together inside Athens, which was not very clean, it is not surprising that people caught diseases. A plague broke out which killed a large number of the inhabitants. The people turned on Pericles, blaming him for their bad luck. He died in 429 BC. Eventually, like two heavyweight boxers who have fought until they are exhausted, both sides were so weak that they made peace in 421 BC.

The Peloponnesian War Part 2: 416-404 BC

One of the many new cities which had sprung up round the Mediterranean was **Syracuse**. Syracuse was the most important city on the island of Sicily. It was rich and magnificent: some called it the 'Athens of the West'. At this time Athens imported all its corn from Sicily and feared the growing power of Syracuse. In 416 BC there was a quarrel between two cities in Sicily: **Selinus**, which was friendly with Syracuse, and **Segesta**, which was friendly with Athens. The people of Segesta sent people to Athens offering to pay for any help the Athenians could give them. The Athenians decided to send an expedition to Sicily. The fleet consisted of one hundred and thirty-four triremes, the latest in warships, and twenty-seven thousand soldiers and sailors. It was under the command of **Nicias**, a politician, **Lamachus**, an experienced general and **Alcibiades**. Alcibiades was a very able young man but he put his own wishes before the good of Athens. Nicias had argued strongly against the expedition but Alcibiades could see only what was in it for himself.

He had been accused of a serious crime and was due to stand trial, but it was decided that he should lead the expedition and stand trial on his return.

No sooner had they arrived in Sicily than a ship arrived from Athens to take Alcibiades back for his trial. After that, everything went wrong. The Athenians were about to capture Syracuse when Lamachus was killed and Nicias became ill. Further bad news arrived: Alcibiades, afraid that he would be found guilty, had escaped from the ship and fled to Sparta. There he betrayed his fellow citizens by telling the Spartans how they could defeat the Athenians. The Spartans arrived in Sicily and beat the Athenians in battle. Many Athenians were killed and most of the survivors were sold as slaves.

The end of the war

Somehow or other the Athenians managed to fight on after this disaster but in the end Sparta and Persia joined together and fought a sea battle against the Athenians at **Aegospotami** in 405 BC. The Athenians were defeated, their city was surrounded and their supply of food was cut off. Athens surrendered and had to give up her empire.

Greek triremes

The huge success which Athens had enjoyed before the Sicilian Expedition was mainly thanks to her navy. Her warships were originally '**penteconters**' (*penteconte* in Greek means fifty) which had a single row of twenty-five oars on each side. In those days, war at sea mostly involved ramming enemy vessels at high speed. The Greeks worked hard to develop a faster ship but one which would not be too long and difficult to control. The result was the '**trireme**' which had three rows of oars. Unfortunately, no triremes of that period have been found and for many years historians argued about how they were built. Some even doubted whether ancient boat-builders could have built such a complicated ship. Then, in the 1980s, following the detailed research of Professor John Morrison, who worked out how the triremes must have been designed, a Greek ship-builder reconstructed a trireme and called it the *Olympias*. The money came from Frank Welsh, a writer and trireme enthusiast. Together they were able to prove that Athenian triremes were manned by a crew sitting at three different levels. With a crew of one hundred and seventy volunteer oarsmen and oarswomen, the *Olympias* in 1988 reached a speed of 9 knots and was able to turn 180 degrees in one minute. The fact that modern human beings are on average 6 cm taller than Ancient Greeks made the conditions cramped and restricted the movements of the inexperienced crew. Probably the ancient crews could have managed to go even faster.

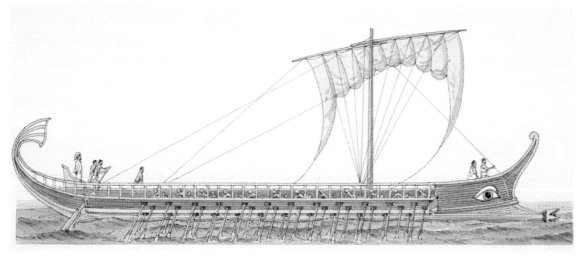

An artist's impression of an Athenian trireme

How do we know?

The story of the Peloponnesian Wars is to be found in *The History of the Peloponnesian War* by the historian **Thucydides**. Thucydides was born between 460 and 455 BC and he was in his twenties when the war began. He himself caught the plague in Athens and describes it in great detail. In 424 BC he was appointed a general and because of a mistake he made, he was exiled from Athens for twenty years. During this time he travelled throughout Greece doing research for what turned out to be his only book.

But historians wanting to learn about Ancient Greece do not rely simply on the writings of historians such as Thucydides or Herodotus. Professor Morrison, for example, as a result of reading a humorous line in a play by Aristophanes, discovered that the oarsmen in a trireme sat on three different levels. Historians are like detectives, and must always be on the look-out for clues.

Exercise 3.1

1. What were the people who lived around Sparta called?

2. How old were Spartan boys when they were taken from their parents?

3. Which three groups of people were not allowed to vote in Athens?

4. On which island did the Confederacy originally keep its money?

5. What was the name of the Athenian who was blamed by the Athenians for the plague?

6. Which city was known as 'the Athens of the West'?

7. In which year did the Battle of Aegospotami take place?

. . . .

Exercise 3.2

Complete the following sentences:

1. The two most powerful cities in 5th century Greece were _____ and _____.

2. The region around Sparta was called _____.

3. Even when they were married, Spartan men couldn't return home until they reached the age of _____.

4. _____ went to Sparta to carry on talks while the walls of Athens were being rebuilt.

5. _____ is the modern name for Corcyra.

6. The Peloponnesian War began in _____ BC.

7. The three commanders of the expedition to Syracuse were _____, _____ and _____.

Exercise 3.3

Explain what is meant by the following:

1. a penteconter
2. a trireme
3. a confederacy

4. helots
5. the Peloponnesian War
6. a plague

Exercise 3.4

Thucydides, who was an Athenian, tells us that the Spartans tried to stop the rebuilding of the walls of Athens after the Persian Wars because they wanted to keep the Athenians weak. Imagine that you are listening to the debate between Themistocles and the Spartans. What arguments might Themistocles have given for rebuilding the walls of Athens, and what might the Spartans have said in reply? Write an account of the debate.

Exercise 3.5

1. Imagine that you are a Spartan boy. You have just reached the age when you must leave home and live in barracks. Write your first letter home, describing your new life.

2. You are a farmer living in Attica and the Spartans are invading. Describe what it is like leaving your farm and living in Athens.

3. Suppose that you are an oarsman on a brand new trireme. Describe the conditions on board. Your trireme attacks a Spartan warship. Say what happens.

Chapter 4
Life in 5th century Athens

Life at home

To understand Greek society it is important to understand what separate lives men and women led. The writer **Xenophon** puts it this way: 'It is better for a woman to remain indoors rather than to be outside, but for the man it is better to take care of affairs outside the house.' A woman was not allowed to go out on her own, and if she did go out it would only be for weddings, funerals or religious services. She would normally stay at home running the house, or spinning or weaving.

In peacetime the man would spend his time at the Assembly or in the Agora, or he might be at the gymnasium or, perhaps, working in the fields. His social life was spent with other men. They would have had the same sort of education as each other, at home and in schools, in oratory, athletics, literature and military service.

When Athens was at war, a man might be away from home as part of the citizen army. A woman was always under the control of a man. Her father controlled her life when she was young and chose a suitable husband for her.

When a young couple married they would hardly know one another. A boy and girl could never go out together, and the few meetings they had before marriage would be strictly supervised by adults. Once married, the wife would manage her husband's house and try to please him by giving him his dearest wish, a male heir.

A couple meeting in ancient Greece, under supervision

Houses

Houses in Athens were built around a courtyard, with stone or clay bricks for the walls and tiles on the roof. They were two storeys high and had an *andron*, a room for men, and a *gynaikeion*, a room for women. In fact, an Athenian house had many rooms in common with a house of today: there was a dining room, kitchen, bathroom and bedrooms. Someone who owned a shop or business would have had a separate workshop or room for trade with access directly from the street. The *andron* was used only by men and here the regular drinking party, or *symposion*, would be held. The guests at these parties ate and drank a great deal, and slaves often had to carry the drinkers home afterwards. Meanwhile the women of the household worked in the *gynaikeion* on the upper floor. The richer women enjoyed activities such as weaving and sewing, while household tasks like cleaning and cooking were usually left to the servants, though it was the woman's role to organise them. Women were only allowed to leave their houses for short periods of time, so they used to enjoy the fresh air in their own private courtyard. The furniture they used was very similar to ours today, and we can easily make out chairs, tables, stools and couches on the pictures they painted on their pottery. The finest and most valuable pieces of furniture were kept in the *thalamos*, or master bedroom. Greek houses were usually simply decorated inside with single colours on the walls, red being particularly popular. The floors were usually tiled or made with flat stones. However, the grander houses, owned by richer citizens, sometimes had a form of mosaic using pebbles and shells to create a picture.

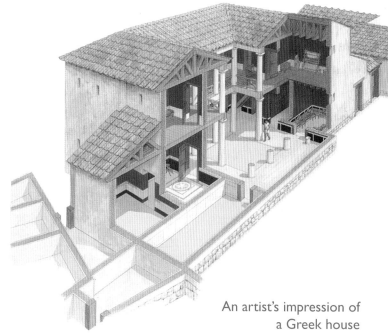

An artist's impression of a Greek house

Politics

Politics was important to the Athenians. Every male citizen who was eighteen years of age or more could go to the Assembly. He had the right to speak and to vote on home or foreign policy.

If there were not enough people at the Assembly, slaves holding ropes soaked in fresh, red paint would run through the Agora, swinging the ropes, and anyone whose clothes had a red mark was made to pay a fine. Magistrates, called *archons*, were not elected but selected 'by lot', which meant that their names were picked at random from those who had put themselves forward. This meant that their elections were fairer and more peaceful. The Athenians were divided into ten tribes. The *Boule*, or Council, consisted of five hundred citizens, fifty from each tribe. These members of the Council didn't stand for election, but were selected by lot from all those who had volunteered. In a similar way, six thousand members of the jury were selected by lot at the beginning of the year to work in the law courts. During a trial, when the prosecutor and the defendant had finished speaking, the jury voted on whether the defendant was guilty or not. If the defendant was guilty, the prosecutor and the defendant both suggested a punishment, and the jury voted again on which one to use. The whole system was an example of good government which few in the ancient world managed to equal.

Architecture

The Parthenon as it is now

The Athenians lived in simple houses and saved the skills of their builders for public buildings and, particularly, temples. These were to be found both in the Agora and on the Acropolis, the sacred rock of Athens, on which Pericles had the **Parthenon** and other beautiful temples built after the Persian Wars. The Parthenon, sacred to the goddess Athene, was made of marble with simple Doric columns, decorated with carvings by the great sculptor **Pheidias**. It contained the great **chryselephantine** statue of Athene which stood 10 metres high. 'Chryselephantine' means 'covered in gold and ivory'.

On the outside, high up above the columns, was a carving called a *frieze*, 1 metre high and 160 metres long, on which was shown the great **Panathenaic procession,** held each year in honour of Athene (see p. 37). Pheidias's work was loved by every Athenian. The Parthenon stood for more than two thousand years until 1684, when the Venetians, in their war against the Ottoman Empire, were trying to remove the Turks from Athens. The Turks were using the Parthenon as a weapons store and a direct hit by the Venetians all but destroyed it. Since then it has been partly rebuilt.

In the Agora, as well as temples there were other buildings, the most famous of which was the *Stoa Poikile*, the 'Painted Stoa'. A *stoa* was a covered walkway with a row of columns on one side and a wall on the other. It was in the open air, but shaded from the sun, a place for men to meet and have long conversations. The Painted Stoa had pictures of great Athenian victories, such as **Marathon**, and contained battle trophies, such as shields taken from a defeated enemy.

There were three main types of column:

- The **Doric** column was the simplest, with no decoration at the base and a capital (top) with a simple circle topped by a square.

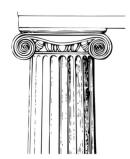

- The **Ionic** column had a base decorated with rings and a capital of simple scrolls.

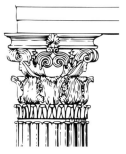

- The **Corinthian** was the most complicated, with its capital decorated with leaves.

Columns supported a horizontal beam and in temples this was topped by a triangular block. The Romans, who copied these Greek columns, made more use of arches which could support heavier and taller walls.

Festivals

There were several religious festivals during the year, but easily the greatest was the **Panathenaic festival**, held each year in honour of Athene. It consisted of contests, processions and sacrifices. Athenians competed with one another in music, athletics, horse racing and boat races. Winners received *amphorae* (enormous jugs) of olive oil which was Athene's special gift to Athens. Olive oil could be used for cooking, lighting, bathing (there was no soap) and massaging the limbs of athletes. At night there was a torch race and the winner's torch would light the fire on Athene's altar. On the last day there was the prize-giving, with feasting and celebration and, most importantly, the procession.

Four girls led the procession, carrying a *peplos*, a garment to place on a life-size statue of Athene on the Acropolis. Behind them came animals, musicians, priestesses, chariots, craftswomen (Athene was their patron), winners of the contests and, at the end, ordinary Athenian citizens. Every fourth year they took a colossal *peplos*, like a sail on a ship, up to the Parthenon to adorn the giant statue of Athene.

The Olympic games

While the Panathenaic festival was the greatest of the Athenian festivals, another that people from all over Greece would have enjoyed was the **Olympic Games**. The first Games we know of were held in 776 BC and continued every four years (or *Olympiad*) until they were cancelled in 393 AD. For the Games, the Greeks declared a sacred truce, a short time when athletes could pass in safety through enemy territory to reach Olympia, a small town in southern Greece. The Games were dedicated to Zeus, whose temple was nearby. Inside the temple was a gigantic chryselephantine statue of Zeus, 12 metres high, which was one of the Seven Wonders of the World. The winning athletes were given wreaths of wild olive from the tree which stood by the temple. All Greeks who were free citizens and hadn't committed murder were allowed to take part. First they had to swear an oath that they had been training for six months and that they would respect the rules of the competitions. The events included running races, boxing, wrestling, chariot racing, horse racing, jumping, discus and javelin. The winner of a contest may only have received an olive wreath but, when he returned home, he was treated like a hero. He was given special privileges, his statue was put up in the Agora and poets would write special poems called *odes* in his honour. The Olympic Games brought all the Greek-speaking peoples together.

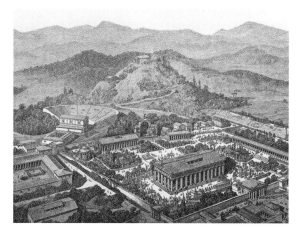 

Artist's impression of Olympia in the 5th century BC   Olympia today

Dates in this book use BC or AD, but the Greeks dated events with reference to Olympiads, for example, 'in the third year of the twentieth Olympiad'. At the end of the 19th century, Baron Pierre de Coubertin decided to restart the Olympic Games. The first Games of modern times took place in Athens in 1896. They included the first marathon race.

Drama

Drama had its origins in religion. Greeks put on plays at festivals dedicated to Dionysus, the god of wine. Only three actors were allowed and they wore masks to represent their characters. Amazingly, plays were written for a single performance only. Nobody expected a repeat. A *chorus* provided background information to the audience. It was happy when good people did well, and was sad when they suffered. The theatre consisted of four main parts. The *theatron*, the place where the audience sat to watch the plays, was curved and set on a hillside. Between the audience and the stage, was the *orchestra*, a circular space where the *chorus* of the play danced and sang its words. Behind the stage, where the three actors performed, was the *skene* (literally 'tent'), where the actors used to change.

The ruins of the theatre at Epidaurus

Painted on the *skene* would be the setting of the play, perhaps a palace or a street. Three playwrights, one for each day of the festival, were chosen to take part in a competition. Each would write three ***tragedies*** and a ***satyr*** play. A *tragedy* is a play in which a hero, almost always one from a myth and well-known to the audience, comes to a sad end. If the three tragedies followed the same story they were called a trilogy. A *satyr* play featured goat-like creatures, connected with the worship of Dionysus, a bit of fun after three tragedies in a row. The ***polis*** (city) chose rich men, called ***choregoi***, to pay for the plays. It was like an extra tax for the wealthiest citizens. Judges decided which of the writers had won the competition. Three of the most successful writers were **Aeschylus**, **Sophocles** and **Euripides**, and many of their plays have survived. While tragedy dealt with the distant past, comedy was right up to date, being written about people or politics of the day. **Aristophanes**, whose comedies we can still read today, made fun of other playwrights, philosophers or politicians. Some of his humour was very rude and the things he wrote about leading citizens must have made him rather unpopular.

How do we know?

We probably know more about Athens in the 5th century BC than anything else in ancient Greek history, because of the large amount of writing that survives from this period. If you ever study Ancient Greek, you will find that the Greek you are reading generally comes from this period. Historians such as **Thucydides** and **Xenophon**, playwrights such as **Aeschylus**, **Sophocles**, **Euripides** and **Aristophanes**, and philosophers such as **Plato** and **Aristotle** all provide us with information about life in Athens during the 5th century BC. In addition to all this we have archaeological evidence. For example, although the procession in the Panathenaic festival is mentioned by several writers, the best evidence we have for how it was organised is the frieze which ran round the outside wall of the Parthenon. When we look at this, we must remember that originally it was painted in bright colours, with swords and other items of real metal. What makes this frieze special is that we see men and gods in the same picture. Normally they were kept separate.

Parthenaic procession: A freize on the Parthenon

As for the Olympic Games, archaeologists have discovered in Olympia fragments of discus, javelin points and even the changing room. Paintings on vases and other pottery show us boxers and sprinters, and even show judges whipping people who have cheated.

Exercise 4.1

1. At what age was a man allowed to go to the Assembly?

2. How many citizens formed the *Boule*?

3. Which three groups of people were not allowed to vote?

4. What is the name of the great temple dedicated to Athene, which is still to be seen on the Acropolis?

5. What does 'chryselephantine' mean?

6. In which year was the Parthenon badly damaged by an explosion?

7. In which year were the first Olympic Games held?

8. What was the prize for the winner of an Olympic event?

Exercise 4.2

Complete the following sentences:

1. In a Greek house the *andron* was reserved for _____.

2. The _____ was the equivalent of the Roman Forum.

3. Athenian magistrates (*archons*) were selected by _____.

4. The Parthenon was built on the _____, the sacred rock of Athens.

5. The simplest and plainest of the three types of column was the _____.

6. The ancient Olympic Games were cancelled in _____ AD.

7. Poets celebrated the fame of the winners of Olympic contest in a special poem called an _____.

8. The _____ danced and sang in the *orchestra*.

Exercise 4.3

Explain what is meant by the following:

1. a *stoa*
2. the capital (of a column)
3. an *amphora*

4. a *peplos*
5. a truce
6. a tragedy

· ·

Exercise 4.4

Study the pictures below:

A.

B.

1. Look at picture A. How do you think the item was used? How useful do you think it was?

2. Look at picture B. How is this scene similar to what you might expect to see today, and how is it different?

Exercise 4.5

1. Imagine that you are taking part in the Olympic games. (You can choose which event you take part in.) Describe what happens, especially when you win!

2. Write about life in Athens from a married woman's point of view.

3. Produce a travel brochure for Athens in the 5th century BC. Describe the city in a way which you think will encourage people to visit. Include pictures or drawings of the main buildings, or design some of your own, showing the three types of column you have learnt about.

Chapter 5
Macedonia and Alexander the Great

The decline of Athens and Sparta

At the end of the Peloponnesian War, the Spartans, who had formed an alliance with the Persians, defeated the Athenians in the Battle of Aegospotami in 405 BC. Athens itself wasn't destroyed but the peace terms were harsh. The Athenians had to give up their empire, lose all but twelve of their warships, destroy the **Long Walls** which joined Athens to its harbour at Piraeus and become an ally of Sparta, their ancient enemy. The **Oligarchs**, the party in Athens which favoured the rule of the few, took advantage of the situation, seized power and murdered many of the **Democrats**, although later (in 403 BC) the Spartans stepped in and restored the Democrats to power.

In 387 BC the Persians made the cities and islands of Greece agree that the Greek cities of Asia Minor, which were the cause of the invasions of 490 and 480 BC, should go back to being ruled by the Persians. To the north of Athens was a town called **Thebes**. Seeing how weak Athens and Sparta had become, the Thebans now felt confident enough to attack the Spartans and they beat them in the Battle of Leuctra in 371 BC under their leader **Epaminondas**. The might of Athens and Sparta was at an end.

Macedonia

In the north of Greece was a country called **Macedonia**. The Macedonians, a fierce, war-like race, thought they were Greek, but the southern Greeks, especially the Athenians, thought they were barbarians. While Athens and Sparta were fighting, Macedonia was growing more and more powerful. **Philip**, their king from 359 BC to 336 BC, introduced the *sarissa*, a pike six metres long, and the *phalanx*, a tight formation of infantry. He had learnt how to fight from Epaminondas when he was being held as a hostage in Thebes. His cavalry included a special group called his **Companions**. His gold mines in Thrace meant that he could afford to build the most powerful army in Greece. He formed alliances with smaller cities round the north of the Aegean and became a real threat to the cities in the south. Some Athenians thought that an alliance with the Macedonians was important, but **Demosthenes**, the greatest speaker Athens ever had, spoke so well against King Philip that the Athenians were determined to resist him. We call these speeches *Philippics*. So, when King Philip marched south, he found an army of Thebans and Athenians facing him. He defeated them in the Battle of Chaeronea (338 BC) and forced all the cities in Greece (except Sparta) to recognise him as their leader. King Philip held a meeting of all the Greek states at Corinth and announced that he was going to lead them all on an invasion of Persia. Then in 336 BC, just as he was about to set out, he was murdered. He was succeeded on the throne by his son **Alexander**.

Alexander the Great: the Persian expedition

Aristotle, Alexander's tutor. A sculpture made in 1754

Alexander was born in 356 BC. He was taught by the great Athenian philosopher Aristotle, and grew up with a love of the Greek way of life.

He was interested in science, medicine and nature and they say that he had a copy of Homer's *Iliad* under his pillow – as well as his dagger! While still a boy, he managed to tame a horse which no-one else could control. The horse had a big, thick head, more like that of a bull, so he called it **Bucephalus** (from the Greek words *bous* = 'bull', *cephale* = 'head'). This was the horse which carried him into battle for many years.

Bucephalus

At the age of sixteen, while his father was away at war, Alexander led the Macedonians to victory in battles against local tribes. So, when he came to the throne at the age of twenty, he was sure he could do the job. He was determined to carry out his father's plan to invade Persia and he spent two years preparing for this great adventure. **Darius III**, King of Persia, was very rich and had a huge army, a sizeable navy and a kingdom which stretched from Asia Minor to India. But the oracle at Delphi had said to Alexander: 'My son, you are invincible!'. He crossed the Hellespont, just as Xerxes had in 480 BC, but in the opposite direction. The first thing he did was to go to **Troy** to see the tomb of **Achilles**. There he stood in silence and wept. When his friends asked him why, he replied that Achilles, his great hero, had achieved so much more than he had.

He then advanced to the River Granicus where he found a Persian army waiting for him on the opposite bank. Without hesitation he spurred Bucephalus forward and charged across the river at the head of his Companions. In his special armour and plumed helmet he was easy to recognise and soon the Persians were concentrating their attack on him. He would have been killed if his friend Cleitus hadn't deflected a Persian sword away from him. The Battle of Granicus ended in victory for Alexander who then found himself master of Asia Minor.

In order to start the march to the east, Alexander then commanded all his forces to meet at **Gordium**, a town in the highlands of **Phrygia**. Here there was an ancient chariot tied up with thick rope. The knot was so complicated that nobody had ever been able to untie it. 'Whoever unties this knot,' said the legend, 'will rule over Asia.' Without hesitation Alexander drew his sword and cut clean through it. Nowadays, if somebody solves an immensely difficult problem in a simple way, we call it 'cutting the Gordian knot'.

Alexander then advanced into Syria. There, at the Battle of Issus (333 BC), he came face to face for the first time with King Darius. Alexander led his Companions in a direct attack on King Darius, who fled from the battlefield, abandoning his mother, wife and children. They were terrified because they thought that Darius was dead and that they would soon suffer a similar fate. On his return from battle, Alexander treated them with great respect. He told them that Darius was still alive and that they had nothing to fear. He next advanced into Egypt where he was made **Pharaoh** (the Egyptian form of king that we learnt about in *Junior History Book 1*) and built a city which was to become very famous. It was called Alexandria.

Alexander the Great: the empire

Alexander now reached the place where Iraq is today. He crossed the river **Euphrates** and came to the river **Tigris**. Here he met King Darius in the Battle of Gaugamela (331 BC). Darius had brought with him his finest cavalry and had chosen a flat battlefield where he could use them most effectively. He had the battlefield cleared of bushes and shrubs so that his chariots with sharp scythes attached to their wheels would be able to turn freely. Darius placed himself at the centre of his battle line with his cavalry. Alexander placed himself on the right, leaving his general **Parmenion** to control the left. Alexander was skilful. He put his men into the shape of a wedge and led the attack straight at Darius in the middle of the Persian army. Darius ran, and Alexander had won another great victory.

A sculpture of
Alexander the Great

Next, Alexander went on to enter the Persian capitals of **Babylon**, **Susa** and **Persepolis**. He took possession of such treasures, Plutarch the historian said, that 'could hardly have been carried by 20 000 mules and 5000 camels.' The defeated King Darius was assassinated by one of his own side and was given a royal funeral by Alexander.

Now Alexander faced some serious problems. He admired the Persians and he wanted to join them with the Greeks into one mighty nation. His fellow Greeks thought the Persians were barbarians and didn't like their foreign ways. They didn't trust the gorgeous robes the Persians wore or the way they bowed down before Alexander. Alexander advanced into India where he came face to face with **King Porus** who hoped to use elephants to bring him victory. Elephants terrify horses, so he put them in front of his troops, hoping that Alexander's cavalry wouldn't dare to approach. However, the Macedonians killed the elephants' drivers from a distance with arrows. The elephants panicked and charged off in all directions, causing havoc in the Indians' ranks. Porus was captured and, when Alexander asked him how he wanted to be treated, he replied proudly, 'As a king!' Alexander not only spared his life but made Porus *satrap*, or governor, of his country.

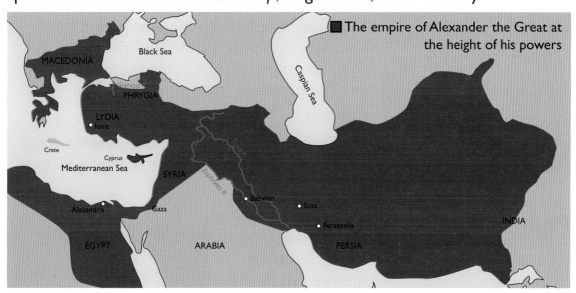

The empire of Alexander the Great at the height of his powers

At this time, Alexander's trusty horse Bucephalus died and a new city of Bucephala was established in his honour. Alexander then wanted to go further east with the expedition, but his followers had been away from home for four years and wanted to return to enjoy the money they had captured. Alexander was forced to give in to the wishes of his men. He ordered them to retreat but, when they reached Babylon in 323 BC, he caught a fever and died, aged thirty-two. As he lay on his death bed, they asked him who he wanted to succeed him. He answered, 'The best man!' and died. He had created a mighty empire that stretched from Greece in the west to the Punjab in India in the east, from the Danube in the north to Egypt in the south.

The legacy of Greece

Alexander had no son and, after his death, rich and powerful men fought over his empire and gradually it broke up. So, was everything that Alexander achieved lost? Is it as if he had never existed? Alexander was brought up to be a Greek. His tutor and the greatest influence on his life was **Aristotle**, the great Athenian philosopher, and through him Alexander developed an interest in the Greeks and, particularly, the Athenians: their science and

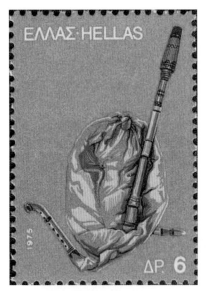

medicine, drama and poetry, philosophy and religion. His empire was not going to last; empires never do. Nevertheless, Greek ideas spread through the known world, and the common language used for trade and communication in all the countries conquered by Alexander was Greek. The next period in history is known as the **Hellenistic Age**. *Hellas* is the Greek word for 'Greece' (you can find it on Greek stamps) and the Greeks called themselves **Hellenes**.

We finish this chapter by looking at some areas where Greek ideas have had a lasting impact.

Philosophy

In 5th century Athens, a man called **Socrates** spent his life looking for wisdom and truth. This was the beginnings of what we now call **philosophy** ('philosophy' is made from two Greek words, *phileo* = 'I love', and *sophia* = 'wisdom'), and people, young people in particular, were interested in what he had to say. He had a peculiar way of passing on his ideas. Instead of giving lectures, he asked questions and, often, people who started with firm beliefs found themselves saying the exact opposite after answering his patient questions. He believed in a single god, an inner voice or

A sculpture of Socrates

conscience, not the gods of the official religion of Athens. As a result he was prosecuted and sentenced to death for 'corrupting the youth of Athens'. Nothing Socrates wrote has survived, but one of his followers was a man named **Plato**, who wrote down the conversations Socrates had with other people. Plato has been given the name 'Father of Modern Philosophy' and Aristotle, one of Plato's students, is known as the 'Father of Modern Science'.

Alexandria

Alexandria, the city founded in Egypt by Alexander, was an example to the world of what the Greeks had achieved. The city was well designed with parallel, linking streets and magnificent architecture.

Its **lighthouse** (*pharos*) was said to be one hundred metres high and became one of the Seven Wonders of the World.

The Library housed the largest collection of manuscripts and books in the ancient world. It became the greatest university of its time with its great Museum, a huge building devoted to the Muses, the nine daughters of Zeus who cared for the Arts and Science. Of these, perhaps the most famous was Clio, the Muse devoted to History.

An artist's impression of the pharos at Alexandria

Mathematics and science

Much of our knowledge of mathematics comes from the work of Greek mathematicians. **Euclid** produced a book of geometry which was used in schools right up to the beginning of the 20th century. **Pythagoras** discovered a rule about the sides of right-angled triangles which we still use. Thales discovered that the moon is lit by the sun, and he could predict eclipses. He also worked out a way of finding the height of a pyramid by measuring shadows. **Aristarchus** produced the startling theory that the Earth rotates round the sun, an idea which didn't catch on until **Copernicus** repeated it almost 2000 years later. But the one we all remember best is **Archimedes**.

Archimedes was asked to discover whether a crown was made of pure gold. He decided to think about it in his bath. As he lowered himself into the bath, the water overflowed and splashed onto the floor. Realising that this showed a way of measuring the volume of a solid object, he leapt from his bath and ran down the street shouting '*Eureka! Eureka!*' ('I have found it!'). Pity he forgot the towel! His most useful invention was **Archimedes's Screw**, still named after him, a method of raising water from rivers for watering fields. He also invented some deadly war machines which were used in the defence of **Syracuse** against the Romans.

What we owe to the Greeks

The British Museum in London

There are so many things which we take for granted without realising that we owe them to the Greeks; important things like **trial by jury**, **theatre** (comedy and tragedy), **democracy** and, of course, the **alphabet**. Some of our grandest architecture, the **British Museum** for example, is copied from the Greeks.

Athletics (a word derived from Greek) and the idea that the ideal education is a blend of intellectual, physical and moral learning, are gifts from the Greeks. The Romans, from the moment that Greece came under their control in 146 BC, were dazzled by the brilliance of Greek culture. Roman architecture, drama, art, philosophy, education, medicine – the list is endless – were almost all copied from the Greeks. Medieval Arab philosophers, mathematicians and scientists, leading thinkers of their time, all studied Aristotle and other Greek thinkers.

How do we know?

In this chapter we have learnt about Alexander the Great, a great hero from history. But how do we know about him? There are five historians who wrote about Alexander the Great. All of them lived at least three centuries after the events they described, but all of them used earlier sources which have since disappeared. They give different descriptions of Alexander. Some say he was a bloodthirsty tyrant, others a saintly character who only wanted harmony and peace. Others say that he was a good man when he started but went downhill when he became more powerful and came under the influence of the Persians. As we are learning, the historian's task is to read all the sources and to think about them in order to come to some conclusion.

Exercise 5.1

1. Who led the Spartans to victory over the Athenians in the Battle of Leuctra?

2. What was a *sarissa*?

3. What do we call the speeches made by Demosthenes against King Philip?

4. In which year did Alexander become king of Macedonia?

5. Who was Alexander's tutor?

6. Who lost the Battle of Issus (333 BC) and ran away?

7. What was the name of Alexander's horse?

8. What is the Greek word for 'Greece'?

Exercise 5.2

Complete the following sentences:

1. The _____ was a tight infantry formation introduced into the Macedonian army by King Philip.

2. In 338 BC King Philip defeated an army of Athenians and Thebans at the Battle of _____.

3. Alexander wept at the tomb of _____ because at his age he hadn't achieved as much as his hero.

4. Solving a difficult problem in a simple way is known as 'cutting the _____ knot'.

5. Alexander defeated King Darius at the Battle of Gaugemela in _____ BC.

6. Alexander died at the age of _____.

7. _____ has been called the 'Father of Science'.

8. The lighthouse which was at Alexandria is called the _____.

. . . .

Exercise 5.3

Explain what is meant by the following:

1. the Oligarchs

2. alliance

3. the Pharaoh

4. a *satrap*

5. philosophy

6. empire

Exercise 5.4

Cleitus, the brother of Alexander's old nurse, once saved the great man's life. Years later at a drunken feast Cleitus started to shout at Alexander. He criticised Alexander's eastern ways and said that King Philip, Alexander's father, was a much greater man. In a fury Alexander threw a spear and killed Cleitus. He then cried until he had no more tears to shed and lay completely still for three days. Some historians have said this shows how cruel Alexander was. Arrian, however, wrote that he thought Cleitus 'deserved the blame for his rudeness' and that Alexander deserved praise for his behaviour.

Write a list of Alexander's good points, and then write a list of his bad points. How do *you* think he deserves to be remembered?

· ·

Exercise 5.5

1. Pretend you are a boyhood friend of Alexander the Great. Write the story of your life, serving with Alexander up to the time of his death.

2. Why do you think Alexander so admired the Greeks?

3. Alexander cried when he stood at the tomb of Achilles. Find out all you can about Achilles and write a story about his life.

Chapter 6
Who were the Romans?

We now go back in time, back to the time of the **Trojan War**, long before the time of the Athenians and Spartans and Alexander the Great that we have been learning about.

The Romans liked to believe that their ancestors were the **Trojans**. In the *Aeneid*, a poem written by the poet **Virgil**, **Aeneas**, a Trojan prince, escaped from Troy while the Greeks were looting and destroying the city. He was carrying his old father on his shoulders and holding his son **Ascanius** by the hand. After many adventures, Aeneas eventually arrived in Italy and built a city called **Lavinium**. His son Ascanius, perhaps wishing to be a king in his own right, built the town of **Alba Longa**. But what about Rome?

Romulus and Remus

Some centuries later, it was believed, a king of Alba Longa called **Procas** died, leaving two sons, **Numitor** and **Amulius**. Numitor became king, but his cruel brother drove him away and killed his son. Amulius then sent Numitor's daughter **Rhea Silvia** to live in the temple sacred to the goddess **Vesta** where she could have no contact with men. He was afraid that she might have sons who would one day try to take his throne. However, **Mars** the god of War came to her and soon afterwards she produced twin sons. Amulius was furious and threw Rhea Silvia into prison; and he ordered her sons to be put in a basket and thrown into the river **Tiber**. Luckily for the twins, the Tiber was in flood and when the waters went down the basket ran aground.

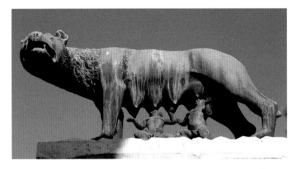

A statue of Romulus and Remus suckling from a she-wolf. Stone Statue made c.1484-96

A she-wolf found the baby boys, but instead of eating them she fed them with her milk. Later a shepherd called **Faustulus** discovered them and took them to his home where he and his wife brought them up as if they were their own children. They called them **Romulus** and **Remus**.

Time passed and they grew up into strong, brave young men who looked after the flocks of Amulius. The shepherds of Amulius's sheep really disliked Numitor's shepherds, and were always fighting with them. One day Remus was captured and taken to Numitor who was, of course, the young man's grandfather. Numitor saw straight away that this was no ordinary country boy, and, after hearing the story of how he had been abandoned as a baby, he was overjoyed to know that his grandchildren had survived. The young men soon removed Amulius from the throne, rescued their mother from her prison and restored Numitor to his kingdom.

The building of Rome, 753 BC

The young men no longer needed to live as shepherds, and they decided to build a new city for themselves. They found an ideal spot by the River Tiber where there were seven hills, but immediately there was an argument. Romulus chose the **Palatine Hill** as the site of the new city, while Remus insisted on the **Aventine Hill**. To settle the matter they decided to leave it to the gods to send them a sign as to which hill to choose. This is called *augury*. Each sat on his favourite hill and waited from early morning until night-fall. Just as it seemed that no sign would come, Remus was thrilled to see six vultures flying home to roost.

The vulture is a sacred bird since it does no harm to living things and so this was taken as a good sign. Remus's joy turned to despair, however, when a messenger arrived to say that Romulus had seen twelve vultures from his hill. So they decided to build the new city on the Palatine Hill. The argument between the brothers had an unhappy ending. When Romulus was building the city wall Remus made fun of it because it was still so low and jumped over it. Romulus angrily attacked his brother and killed him. The city was called 'Rome' after its founder.

The Sabine women

Many men came to live in Rome, some of whom had been thrown out of other cities. These men needed wives, so Romulus asked the people of neighbouring cities to let their daughters marry the new Romans. They refused to allow their daughters to marry such ruffians. Romulus now thought of a cunning plan. He invited the **Sabines**, Rome's nearest neighbours, to a celebration. There would be a feast and games and a chance to look at the new city. The Sabines arrived, whole families of them, unarmed and unsuspecting. At a given signal the Romans drew the weapons they had hidden under their tunics and chased away the men and the older women. They didn't allow the young girls to escape but kept them as their wives.

Tarquinius Superbus

Romulus was the first king of Rome. He was followed by six others, the last three of whom were **Etruscans**, the most powerful race in Italy at that time. The seventh and last was **Tarquinius** who was given the name *Superbus* which means 'arrogant' or 'proud' in Latin. He stole from men he hated or suspected of plotting against him and either sent them away or killed them. Tarquinius Superbus was very superstitious. Once, when he was sacrificing to the gods, he saw a serpent on the altar, eating the food which had been offered to the gods. He sent his two sons to **Delphi** to find out the meaning of this sign. With them went their cousin **Brutus** who

pretended to be stupid and clumsy in order to avoid the king's anger. 'Tarquinius will soon lose his throne,' said the oracle. 'Which of us will rule in his place?' asked the sons eagerly. 'The one who is first to kiss his mother,' came the reply.

As they were leaving the temple, Brutus pretended to stumble and, as he fell, he kissed the earth. The young princes laughed at him, not realising that 'Mother Earth' is the mother of us all.

The Republic

When his sons and Brutus returned to Rome, Tarquinius was away at war. At this time the people in Rome were angry because **Sextus**, Tarquinius's son, had treated a lady called **Lucretia** so badly that she had killed herself. When he found out, Brutus stirred up the citizens and when Tarquinius returned he found the city gates locked against him by the angry people.

The Romans swore that they would never again allow themselves to be ruled by one man. Instead they set up what is called a **republic**, a government without kings or queens, where the people choose or *elect* their leaders. The republic was ruled by two men called *consuls*. Other officers (called *magistrates*) were elected yearly to carry out other duties. To begin with, only a few people were allowed to vote, but, as the centuries passed, more and more men were able to do so.

Lars Porsenna

Tarquinius and his son Sextus were desperate to have their kingdom back and went to **Lars Porsenna**, the king of a town called Clusium, to ask for his help. The people of Clusium and of other towns in the region were Etruscans: we now call that part of Italy **Tuscany**. King Porsenna sent messages to all his allies and soon a mighty army had assembled. The Romans worked desperately to fortify their city, especially the **Janiculum**, a hill which was joined to the city by a single wooden bridge. People from all around Rome came hurrying into the city for safety, bringing with them their farm animals and all they could carry. Meanwhile, the huge Etruscan army had captured the Janiculum, in spite of all the Romans' efforts.

Horatius

The consuls called an emergency meeting to discuss what was to be done. There wasn't time to cut down the bridge before the enemy reached it. Then a captain in the army called **Horatius Cocles** stepped forward. 'The approach to the bridge on the other side is very narrow,' he said. 'Three men could hold the enemy back while the rest are cutting down the bridge. I need two volunteers.' Two brave men, **Spurius Lartius** and **Titus Herminius**, stepped forward and crossed with Horatius to the other bank. Everyone else, consuls mixing with common soldiers, took up crow-bars and axes and hacked away at the bridge.

The Etruscans at first were amazed that only three men should resist their mighty army and they made fun of Horatius and his companions. Three Etruscan champions stepped forward but, after a short fight, they lay dead. Others took their place, but the same thing happened. The three Roman

heroes stood their ground, not giving in despite their serious wounds. Then they heard the loud sound of wood creaking and splintering and the voices of their friends calling them back. The bridge was about to fall into the Tiber. Spurius and Titus sprinted back, feeling the timbers cracking under their feet. When they reached safety, they looked back and saw Horatius alone, one man against thirty thousand. They would have returned to his side but, at that moment, the bridge fell with a mighty crash into the water. It lay for a while like a dam with the water building up behind it. Then it was carried away in the flow, leaving Horatius stranded. Lars Porsenna was very impressed by Horatius's bravery and he called on him to surrender. Horatius seemed not to hear and turned towards the river. Saying a short prayer to **Father Tiber**, the god of the river, he dived, wounded and fully armed, into the water. For a time he disappeared from sight. When he surfaced again, the Romans sent up a great shout of triumph and even the watching Etruscans were relieved to see him safe.

Gaius Mucius

Lars Porsenna had been delayed but he stayed on, using the Janiculum as his base, and preventing supplies of food from reaching the city. The Romans were trapped. A young man called **Gaius Mucius** volunteered to enter the Etruscan camp and kill Lars Porsenna. He crept into the Etruscan camp but, not knowing which was the king, he killed the wrong man. He was arrested and taken to Porsenna, who threatened him with dreadful torture if he didn't answer his questions.

Mucius said nothing. He walked to the altar and thrust his right hand into the flame which was burning there. He showed no pain and the king was impressed by his courage. A little later, Lars Porsenna made peace with the Romans and withdrew from their territory, leaving behind supplies of food for the starving Romans. Gaius Mucius was praised by the Romans for his courage and, because of the injury he had suffered in the flames, was given the name *Scaevola*, which means 'left-handed'.

How do we know?

A great deal of the early history of Rome is legendary. Nobody nowadays would believe the story of Romulus and Remus. The stories in this chapter about Lars Porsenna, Horatius and Mucius Scaevola read more like an adventure story than real history. So, can they be true?

What we do know is that wars did take place between the Romans and the Etruscans, even if we are not sure about the details. The historian **Livy** wrote an enormous book called *Ab Urbe Condita*, which means 'From the foundation of the city', a history of Rome from its beginning right up to his day. He was writing more than seven hundred years after the building of Rome but the Romans adored these stories. They gave them a sense of pride in their ancestors, and they passed them down to their children and grandchildren.

. . . .

Exercise 6.1

1. Who wrote the *Aeneid*?

2. What was the name of Numitor's brother?

3. What is the name of the river which flowed through Rome?

4. In which year was Rome built?

5. How many vultures did Romulus see?

6. How many kings of Rome were there?

7. What was the name of the brave soldier who defended the bridge?

. . . .

Exercise 6.2

Complete the following sentences:

1. Aeneas escaped from the city of _____.

2. Ascanius, the son of Aeneas, built the city of _____.

3. A _____ found the babies, Romulus and Remus, and fed them with her milk.

4. _____, a shepherd, discovered the twins and brought them up as his own children.

5. To get themselves wives, the Romans took the daughters of the _____.

6. Tarquinius's nephew, _____, pretended to be clumsy and stupid.

7. When the last king had been expelled, the Romans elected two _____ every year.

8. _____ was the king of Clusium.

Exercise 6.3

Explain what is meant by the following:

1. augury

2. exile

3. *Superbus* (describing Tarquinius)

4. a republic

5. allies

Exercise 6.4

The story of Gaius Mucius is found in the works of Livy. Other historians, **Dionysus of Halicarnassus** and **Plutarch**, tell the same story, that Lars Porsenna didn't in fact capture Rome. The historian **Tacitus**, however, wrote in his *Histories* that the Romans had in fact surrendered to Lars Porsenna, and later historians have also taken that view. Can you think of any reasons which might make us accept one version rather than the other?

Exercise 6.5

1. Tell in your own words the story of Romulus and Remus from the time of their birth to the time when they began to build the city of Rome.

2. You are Horatius Cocles and you are at the consuls' emergency meeting. Write an account of what happens from then on.

3. Tell the story of Gaius Mucius.

Chapter 7
Life in the Republic

Roman religion

Early on in their history the Romans worshipped the same gods as other tribes in Italy living around them. They believed that they were surrounded by spirits, called *numina*, which would help them if they gave them **offerings** (or **sacrifices**).

There were festivals throughout the year. For example, the *Lupercalia* was celebrated in February to encourage crops to grow later in the year. The *Saturnalia*, in honour of the god Saturn, took place in December and as the years went by it expanded until it was a week long. It was rather like our Christmas, not only a religious festival but also a time to eat, drink and be merry. Everyone was on holiday, including the slaves who were allowed to gamble and even to be cheeky to their masters.

Ancestor worship was an important part of Roman religion. A Roman liked to trace his family back for centuries and would display images of his ancestors on the wall just as people nowadays like to show paintings or photographs of their families. In the home there was an altar to the household gods, the *Lares* and *Penates*, and every day the family, led by the head of the household, the *paterfamilias*, would pay their respects to these gods with a small ceremony. For example, **Janus**, the god represented with two heads, was the god of entrances and exits. *ianua* in Latin means 'door', and the month of January comes from his name. The main room in the house, the *atrium* ('hall'), had a fireplace, or hearth, where a fire would burn in cold weather. **Vesta** was the goddess of the hearth and home.

Gradually, as Rome grew and the Romans came into contact with the world outside Italy, they saw that the Greeks had statues of their gods in human form. The Romans already had a supreme god called Jupiter and, because the Greeks' Zeus did similar things, the two became confused in people's minds. In a similar way Aphrodite and Venus, Hermes and Mercury, and many others were thought to be the same.

Roman name	Description	Greek equivalent
Jupiter	ruler of the gods	Zeus
Juno	queen of the gods	Hera
Neptune	god of the sea	Poseidon
Pluto	god of the underworld	Hades
Minerva	goddess of wisdom and the arts	Athene
Diana	goddess of hunting and the moon	Artemis
Apollo	god of music, archery and the sun	Apollo
Venus	goddess of love and beauty	Aphrodite
Mars	god of war	Ares
Bacchus	god of wine	Dionysus
Vulcan	god of fire and metalwork	Hephaestus
Ceres	goddess of the harvest	Demeter
Vesta	goddess of the hearth and home	Hestia
Mercury	messenger of the gods	Hermes

One way of finding out what these gods were planning was to use **augury**, the prediction of the future by signs. For example in 249 BC the Roman admiral Publius Claudius Pulcher was told, shortly before the Battle of Drepana, that the sacred chickens wouldn't eat. This was a bad omen. 'Then let them drink!' he said and had them thrown into the sea. He lost the battle to the Carthaginians and ninety-three of his ships were sunk.

The Republic

After they had driven Tarquinius Superbus out of the city, the Romans, determined never again to be subject to a wicked king, set up the **Republic**. With a republic, people could choose their own leaders. Each year they held elections to choose the two **consuls** who held office for one year. When

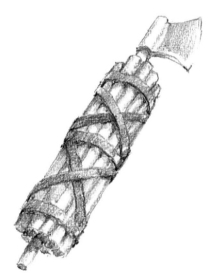

Fasces

they made important decisions, the consuls had to agree with one another. If one consul didn't approve of a decision he had the right of *veto*, meaning he could block what the other consul was trying to do. The consuls had ivory thrones. They had attendants called *lictors* who carried *fasces*, bundles of wooden rods tied round an axe. These were the symbols of their power to punish wrong-doers; the rods showed that they had the right to beat criminals, the axe showed that they could execute them. Many centuries later, Mussolini, the Italian leader who ruled Italy during the Second World War, adopted the *fasces* as the symbol of his political party. It was known as the Fascist Party.

Elections were also held for other important posts and the ambitious young Roman had to try for each of them in turn. He couldn't stand for the consulship until he had been a *quaestor*, who dealt with financial matters and organised public games, then an *aedile*, in charge of public buildings and food and water supplies, and finally a *praetor* who organised the legal system and was himself a judge. This career path was known as the *cursus honorum*, a sort of ladder to the top which had to be climbed rung by rung. The holders of all these various offices were known as *magistrates*.

Patricians and plebeians

A famous abbreviation, always seen on flags and banners in films about ancient Rome, is **SPQR**. This stands for **S**enatus **P**opulus**q**ue **R**omanus, the 'Senate and People of Rome'.

The **Senate** was a group of the heads (*patres* or 'fathers') of the leading families in Rome who met to talk about important political matters. It didn't pass laws but its advice was offered to the consuls and other magistrates who usually accepted it. Roman society consisted of two classes: '**patricians**', from the Latin *patres*, who came from rich land-owning families and could claim ancestors going back to the very foundation of Rome, and '**plebeians**', that is everybody else except, of course, the slaves, who had no rights at all.

The plebeians would be people like farm workers, craftsmen, shopkeepers and newcomers to Rome. Plebeians sometimes became very rich, but they still didn't have the same rights as the patricians who naturally wanted to keep these for themselves. Over the centuries the plebeians fought to win the rights they felt they deserved. For example, plebeians originally were not allowed to marry patricians or to stand for the consulship. They had their own assemblies but they couldn't be senators.

The plebeians go on strike

When Rome went to war, the plebeians were expected to drop everything and fight Rome's enemies. For farmers, this meant leaving their land for months at a time, often causing them to miss the harvest and leave their farms to become overgrown with weeds. No harvest meant no food, so they had to borrow money from the patricians. Later, if they were unable to pay it back, they were forced to work as slaves for the patrician who had lent them the money. Eventually, in 494 BC, when summoned to fight, they refused and withdrew to a hill near Rome, threatening to build a new city.

Meneius Agrippa talking to the plebians

A wise and popular patrician called **Menenius Agrippa** was sent to talk to them. He pointed out that Rome was like a human body, made up of many parts, and that, just as a body needs all its parts to work properly, so Rome would die unless the patricians and the plebeians worked together. He promised that those who had become slaves would be freed. The plebeians returned to Rome and the hill was given the name *Mons Sacer*, the 'Holy Mountain'. In 471 BC the plebeians were given the right to elect officers, called **Tribunes of the Plebs**, to protect them. Much later plebeians were given the right to stand for the consulship. Later still, by law, one of the consuls *had* to be a plebeian and, when his consulship was over, he entered the Senate.

Roman education

In early Rome, children were educated by their parents at home. Mothers would teach their daughters skills which they would need in later life: cooking, weaving, sewing, spinning and other household arts. Fathers would teach their sons reading, writing and all the Roman traditions and history they would need to know in later life. These traditions were referred to as the *mos maiorum*, 'the custom of the elders'. He would also learn how to farm, so that he could take over the running of the family's estates when he grew up. Of course, the education a boy received would depend very much on how much money the family had.

A frieze depicting a school in ancient Rome

Later, schools developed along Greek lines. Greek tutors and schoolmasters were employed to teach young boys how to read, write and count. All educated Romans would have Greek as their second language after Latin. From the age of seven, a boy would go to school with a slave called a **paedagogus** ('tutor'). He would start lessons very early, sometimes before sunrise, and work until lunch-time. He would return home for lunch and a siesta and then go back to school in the late afternoon. All schools charged fees, so very poor children wouldn't be able to go. The children wrote on wax tablets, called **cerae** or **tabulae**, using a **stilus** which was shaped like a pen with a sharp end to make marks on the wax, and a blunt end to smooth out mistakes. The tablets could be used over and over again. They also used pens made out of reed and dipped these in ink wells to write on paper, called **papyrus**.

They read from scrolls, long rolls of papyrus which had to be rewound for the next reader. For counting they used an abacus or pebbles. Some schoolmasters became famous for their fierce discipline. They would beat boys who were naughty or didn't learn their lessons. The tutor too, if he discovered his boy had misbehaved, beat him and so, probably, would the father when the boy got home. At the age of twelve, the boy would go to a grammar school where he would learn Greek and Latin literature. The sons of the richest citizens would then go on to a rhetoric school where they would learn *oratory*, the art of speaking well, an essential skill for a young man who was going to be a lawyer or politician.

The Latin language

The Latin language, originally spoken by the Romans, spread as Roman influence increased in the world until it became the official language of the whole Roman Empire. Then, when the Roman Empire came to an end, the language developed in different ways in different parts of the world until it became Italian, Spanish, French, Portuguese and Romanian. We call these **Romance languages** and they all share the same link with the Romans. English is not considered a Romance language, but around half of our words do come from Latin. We can 'work together' or we can 'collaborate' (*laborare* = 'to work'). To be answerable is to be 'responsible' (*respondere* = 'to answer'). We can be blunt and call a man 'drunk' or we can say that he is 'inebriated' (*ebrius* = 'drunk').

Even after Latin was no longer spoken, it became the common language (*lingua franca*) for scholars, scientists and politicians in Western Europe. The Roman Catholic Church used Latin in its services until fairly recently. In the 1990s churchmen gave up the use of Latin in their conversations but Pope Benedict XVI wants to bring Latin back and speaks it fluently. Latin is still very much alive and around us, not least in the large number of proverbs and phrases that are often used: *carpe diem* ('seize the day'), *dum spiro, spero* ('while I breathe, I hope') and *ad infinitum* ('going on and on'). Even common abbreviations such as 'etc.' (*et cetera* = 'and other things') and 'i.e.' (*id est* = 'that is') are from Latin.

How do we know?

Much of what we know about Roman history and politics we have learned from Livy, the great historian who lived from 59 BC to 17 AD. Unfortunately, less than half of his massive life work of one hundred and forty-two volumes has survived. As well as Livy, there is another great historian of this period. **Polybius** (200-118 BC) was a Greek who was sent to Rome, where he was kept for seventeen years. However, because he was an educated man, he was welcomed into the houses of the top people in Rome and enjoyed their company. He wrote a history of forty books of which only five survive. Livy used his work as a source and it was thought that Polybius tried hard to be accurate and truthful. Because he was a Greek and wrote in Greek, some people believe that he was less biased than Roman historians. Is that necessarily true?

Unless written works were copied and recopied, they could easily disappear because the papyrus on which they were written was fragile and could easily be destroyed by insects, fire or damp. Luckily we do have other evidence in the form of inscriptions carved on stone, which were more likely to survive. The careful work of some scholars has produced a great collection of these, over 180 000 of them, in a book called *Corpus Inscriptionum Latinarum* (a body of Latin inscriptions). From these, scholars can fill in the gaps left by the Roman historians.

. . . .

Exercise 7.1

1. What were the *Lares* and *Penates*?

2. Which Roman god was the equivalent of the Greek god Hermes?

3. Who was the Roman god of war?

4. What did a *praetor* do?

5. In which year did the plebeians withdraw to a hill near Rome and refuse to fight?

6. What name was given to the hill?

7. What was the second language of educated Romans?

8. What were *cerae* used for?

9. What is oratory?

· ·

Exercise 7.2

Complete the following sentences:

1. The head of the household was called the _____.

2. _____ was the goddess of the hearth and home.

3. Bundles of wooden rods, carried by the *lictors*, were called _____.

4. Roman society consisted of two classes, the _____ and the _____.

5. The *paedagogus* was the children's _____.

6. To help them to count, children used an _____ or pebbles.

7. At the age of _____ boys would go to a grammar school.

8. Italian, Spanish, French, Portuguese and Romanian are known as _____ languages.

· ·

Exercise 7.3

Explain what is meant by the following:

1. *numina*

2. *fasces*

3. the right of *veto*

4. the *lictors*

5. the *cursus honorum*

6. *SPQR*

7. *mos maiorum*

8. a *stilus*

Exercise 7.4

Study the pictures below and on the next page:

A.

B.

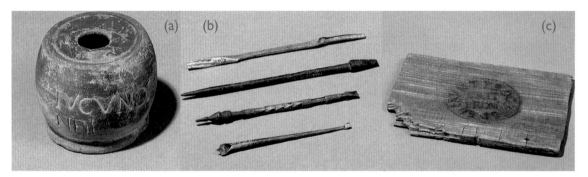

C.

D.

1. Look at Picture A. It shows four stages in a Roman boy's childhood. Can you identify them? Which of these stages are the same and which are different from the childhood of a boy living today?

2. Look at Picture B. Identify the items labelled (a) to (c) and say how each was used.

3. Look at Picture C. What type of scene do you think this portrays?

4. Look at Picture D. What, if anything, does this teach us about Roman education? Think carefully about your answer.

. . . .

Exercise 7.5

1. Imagine that you are Menenius Agrippa. Write about the day you went to the mountain and tried to persuade the plebeians to return to the city.

2. Describe a day at a Roman school, starting in the early morning. You can compare it with the sort of day you have in your school.

3. Here is a list of Latin words. They are all parts of the body. Try to find English words which come from them. Some of the words have two parts and, if so, you should use the second part.

   caput, capitis = head; *digitus* = finger; *oculus* = eye; *pes, pedis* = foot; *os, oris* = mouth; *collum* = neck; *manus* = hand.

4. Beneath the great dome in St Paul's Cathedral (built, as you will know, by Sir Christopher Wren) is a simple Latin inscription: '*si monumentum requiris, circumspice*'. Tourists who are looking for Wren's tomb should read the inscription. What does it mean? Here are some words which may help you: *si* = if; *circum* = around; *spice* = look. Note that *–is* on the end of a verb means 'you'.

Chapter 8
Rome's domination of Italy

Rome was the main city in the region of Italy called **Latium**. The people who lived there were called the *Latini*, or Latins. After they had driven out King Tarquinius in 509 BC, they first had to deal with the Etruscans. They joined with the Latins, and made the **Latin League**, and during the 5th and 4th centuries BC they drove the Etruscans out of Latium. In 387 BC Gauls poured across the Alps from the region we call France and captured Rome. They weren't interested in settling in Rome. They looted the city and returned across the Alps. In 340 BC the Latins rose up against the Romans because they felt they were too powerful in the Latin League. However, the Romans defeated the Latins, broke up the League and found themselves in control of Latium.

The Samnites

The **Samnites** were a tribe of warriors and herdsmen who lived in the hills of central Italy. They came down from the hills with their herds into the plain, attacking the people who lived there and seizing their homes. In 343 BC they attacked the city of **Capua**, which asked Rome for help. The Romans went to the rescue and the war with the Samnites went on, with two breaks, from 343-290 BC. The Romans eventually won and gained control of most of Italy. Only the Greek cities in the south (so called because the inhabitants had settled there from Greece) remained outside Roman control.

The Pyrrhic War

Tarentum was one of these cities and, when it attacked and captured **Thurii**, a town friendly to Rome, **Aemilius** the consul was sent with his legions to demand the return of Thurii. The Tarentines refused and sent messengers to **Epirus** in Greece to ask for the help of King **Pyrrhus**. He arrived with his army and twenty elephants. He had learnt from the Carthaginians how useful elephants could be in battle.

In the fierce battle which followed, it looked as if the Romans were going to win, but Pyrrhus brought forward his elephants. Their trumpeting terrified the Roman horses which charged wildly off, scattering their own foot soldiers. Pyrrhus was victorious; but when Pyrrhus saw how many men his victory had cost him, he said that, if he won another victory like that, he would be returning to Epirus alone. Today, when we say that someone has won a 'pyrrhic victory', we mean that it has been won at too great a cost. Pyrrhus won another victory against the Romans, but again he lost too many men. When the Romans finally forced him to go back to Greece, they now found themselves in control of the whole peninsula of Italy.

The Roman army

The main reason the Romans were so successful was their army. The army was made up of *legions*. There were about six thousand men in each one. The legion was divided into ten *cohorts* and each cohort was made up of six *centuries*. Eight legionaries shared a tent and ten tents made a century, eighty men in all, under the command of a *centurion*. Attached to the legion were the cavalry and sometimes there were other soldiers who were non-citizens

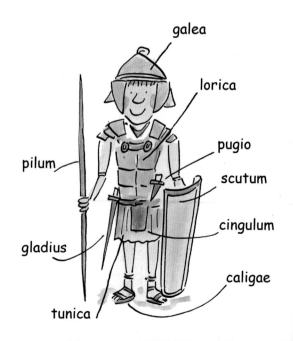

galea

lorica

pugio

scutum

cingulum

caligae

pilum

gladius

tunica

who came from outside Italy. These *auxiliaries* were often specialists such as archers and slingers. The legionary soldier had to be able to march more than thirty kilometres in a day carrying not only his weapons but food and camping equipment. When he arrived at the site of that night's camp, he had to help to build it, digging ditches and making earth walls. He had a metal helmet, armour made of overlapping iron bands, a short sword for stabbing, and a rectangular shield. He also had to carry a throwing spear called a *pilum*. Each cohort had its own standard while the legion had its *aquila* ('eagle'). To lose that eagle to the enemy was the worst thing that could happen to the legion. A legionary had to serve for at least twenty-five years. At the end of that time he would receive a small sum of money and perhaps a piece of land.

Carthage

Carthage was built on the north coast of Africa in 814 BC by **Phoenicians** who came from the east coast of the Mediterranean. The wars between the Romans and the Carthaginians are called the **Punic Wars**, a name which comes from the Latin word for Phoenician.

The first Punic War, 264-241 BC

The Carthaginians were a race of people who travelled throughout the world buying and selling. Both they and the Romans wanted control of Sicily. Sicily was famous for its corn and both Rome and Carthage needed more and more corn to make bread for their people. When the Carthaginians raided towns in Sicily, burning houses and selling the inhabitants into slavery, the Romans declared war on them. The Roman army was able to drive the enemy away, but the Romans realised that they would never win totally as long as the Carthaginians had a more powerful fleet of warships than their own. These warships were called **quinqueremes** (Latin *quinque* = 'five', *remus* = 'oar'), similar to the triremes we learnt about in Chapter 3, but with five banks of oars or possibly five rowers to each oar; nobody is certain which. By chance the Romans found one of the enemy ships grounded on a shore. They took it away and, using it as a pattern, built one hundred and twenty of them in a very short time. While this was happening, they needed trained oarsmen for their new fleet. They arranged banks of benches on hillsides and taught crews of rowers the skills they needed.

Although they had this new fleet of ships, the Romans still thought like soldiers. They had a gang-plank with a spike which was let down when they came near an enemy ship. The spike stuck in the deck and the Romans ran over the plank and fought the enemy hand to hand. In 260 BC the two fleets met. The Carthaginians were led by a brilliant general called **Hamilcar Barca** but despite his efforts, the Romans won a great victory. After more than twenty years the Romans were victorious.

The second Punic War, 219-202 BC

Hamilcar Barca had a son called **Hannibal**. When he was nine years old, Hannibal begged to be allowed to go with his father to war. His father, who was sacrificing to the gods at an altar, made him swear that he would always be an enemy to the Romans. When both Hamilcar and Hannibal's elder brother **Hasdrubal** were dead, Hannibal was put in charge of the army at the age of twenty-six. In Spain, Hannibal besieged **Saguntum**, an ally of Rome, and captured it. **Cornelius Scipio**, a Roman general, was sent to Spain to punish Hannibal but Hannibal had already begun a journey which would take him across the Alps and into Italy. Across the Alps! Was Hannibal brave or foolish to lead an army which included elephants over the Alps?

Snow had already fallen when the Carthaginians reached the Alps. The path they followed was narrow and slippery and the natives of the region kept attacking them with arrows and huge boulders. Pack horses which were hit by the arrows ran away and fell to their deaths in the crevasses below. The soldiers suffered from frostbite. After nine days they reached the summit and Hannibal tried to encourage his men by pointing to Italy. 'There is the way that leads to Rome,' he said. But the way down the mountains was every bit as dangerous as the way up and Hannibal arrived in Italy with only twenty-six thousand men left of the forty-six thousand who had started out.

The Battle of Lake Trasimene, 217 BC

Hannibal now started on the road which led to Rome and before long reached **Lake Trasimene**. Between the lake and the mountains was a road which Hannibal saw as an ideal place for an ambush. He positioned his men above the road and waited. A thick mist had risen from the lake and the Romans marched unsuspecting into the trap. The Carthaginians above the road were in bright sunshine and fired their arrows and threw their spears down onto the Romans below. Hannibal's infantry and cavalry attacked and the Roman army was destroyed. Of the thirty-six thousand Romans only six thousand survived. The rest were either killed or drowned as they tried to escape in their heavy armour. When the news arrived in Rome, everyone was very sad. '*Pugna magna victi sumus,*' said the Praetor. 'We have been defeated in a great battle.'

The Romans decided to appoint **Quintus Fabius** as **Dictator** to save them from the danger posed by Hannibal. (A dictator was a man appointed in times of great danger who had the power to control the whole country as necessary.) Quintus Fabius knew that Hannibal couldn't be beaten in open battle, so he followed Hannibal at a distance, only attacking small bands of Carthaginians when they were separated from the main army. For this strategy he became known as *Cunctator*, the 'Delayer'. Later, when the Romans understood better what he had done, they called him Quintus Fabius **Maximus** (*maximus* = 'greatest').

The Battle of Cannae, 216 BC

The Romans, worried because Hannibal was still a threat, elected two new consuls and Fabius resigned his dictatorship. The consuls led their eight legions, the largest Roman army ever, to a place called **Cannae** and joined battle with the Carthaginians. The result was a complete disaster for Rome. Only a few thousand Romans escaped; the rest were cut to pieces or taken prisoner. One of Hannibal's officers, **Maharbal**, begged to be allowed to advance on Rome. Hannibal refused. Maharbal said, 'You know how to win a victory, but not how to use it!'

Hannibal remained in Italy for another thirteen years but he won no more great victories. Eventually, the Carthaginians called him back to Carthage in 203 BC. Encouraged by this, a young general called Scipio landed in Africa and defeated the Carthaginians in the **Battle of Zama** (202 BC). The Romans made the Carthaginians give up their prisoners, their ships (all but ten) and all their land outside Africa. A few years later the Carthaginians again worried the Romans. The Romans attacked again and, after a long siege, Carthage was at last destroyed.

Pompey, Caesar and Crassus: the first triumvirate, 60 BC

During the next hundred years the Romans' power in the world kept growing, but at the same time there were arguments and bloodshed in Rome. Many countries became provinces in the growing Roman Empire, but in Rome itself the Senate cruelly removed anyone who resisted its power. Two brothers, **Tiberius** and **Gaius Gracchus,** saw that farmland was being snatched by rich men to make huge estates, worked by slaves, while the poor, now without their farms, were coming to Rome to look for jobs but not finding any. Because they tried to introduce laws to give the land back to the poor, each in his turn was killed by agents of the Senate.

Later **Marius**, a successful general who was popular with the people, kept the consulship for years. While he was fighting wars abroad, his rival, **Sulla**, seized power. Marius returned and, in five violent days, put Sulla's supporters to death. When Marius died, Sulla returned and murdered his political rivals. He became Dictator in 81 BC but died in 78 BC. Then three men stepped forward who would change the way Rome was run forever.

Pompey

In 80 BC a young general called **Pompey** won such wonderful victories that his soldiers named him *Magnus*, 'the Great'. In 67 BC he was given command of an army whose task was to rid the Mediterranean of pirates. These pirates had taken control of the seas and had more than a thousand ships. He completed the task inside a year and in 66 BC he took charge of the legions in Asia Minor. He added **Syria** and **Judaea** to the Roman empire. He returned to Italy and dismissed

Pompey the Great

his army before he set foot on Italian soil, as the law required. He had promised to give his soldiers land as a reward but the Senate would not let him. He was disappointed and joined with two other powerful politicians, **Crassus** and **Julius Caesar**, who also felt that the Senate was standing in their way. This alliance of the three men is known as a *triumvirate*, from the Latin *trium*, 'of three' and *viri*, 'men'. To hold the group together, Pompey married Caesar's daughter.

Crassus and Spartacus

Crassus was very rich. He had made his money from slaves, silver and houses. He was upset because the Senate would not let him collect taxes in the East. He became famous because he ended a revolt of gladiators led by a gladiator called **Spartacus**.

Gladiators were prisoners who fought to amuse the public. They were so popular that rich citizens set up schools to train gladiators in the different ways of fighting. The conditions in these schools were harsh, and one day a band of gladiators led by Spartacus escaped from their school in Capua. The Romans sent two armies to deal with them but both armies were defeated.

A sculpture of Marcus Licinius Crassus made c 53 BC

Crassus trained the soldiers who had survived the defeat. With this army he built fortifications and ditches to trap the gladiators in southern Italy. Spartacus and a few others managed to escape but Crassus had won a great victory. In all, twelve thousand were killed. Spartacus fought another great battle but, when he found himself surrounded, he killed his horse to show that he wasn't going to run away. Many gladiators were killed. To warn other slaves not to challenge the power of Rome, six thousand survivors, including Spartacus, were crucified along the Appian Way, the main road leading into Rome.

Julius Caesar

Julius Caesar was a young general. He was put in charge of the army in Spain and succeeded in everything he did. When he returned to Italy, it was election time. He wanted to become a consul and to be a candidate he had to enter Rome. He also wanted a *triumph*, which was an honour received by a successful military leader, but to win a triumph he had to remain outside Rome until the Senate agreed to give it to him. Ambitious for power rather than glory, he gave up the triumph and became consul. After his consulship, he demanded to be put in charge of Gaul not for one year, which was the custom, but for five. With Pompey and Crassus to support him, Caesar was now a powerful man and the Senate couldn't refuse.

A sculpture of Gaius Julius Caesar

Caesar in Gaul

Caesar's first task in Gaul was to fight against the **Helvetii**, a tribe who lived in what we now call Switzerland. They had decided to move into Gaul where they would drive out any Gauls who were settled and civilised and friends of Rome. Caesar defeated them and drove them back to their homes. He then took on another tribe, the **Sequani**, led by **Ariovistus**, who were threatening the **Aedui**, a tribe friendly to the Romans. He defeated them in a single battle. He was a superb leader famous for his speed in moving his troops from one place to another. They would advance enormous distances by forced marches and take the enemy by surprise. When he had conquered almost every part of Gaul, he had to face one final revolt.

Vercingetorix, leader of the **Arverni**, called on all the tribes of

A statue of Vercingetorix made in the 19th century

Gaul to join forces against Caesar. He seized **Gergovia**, the capital city of the region, and managed to resist every effort Caesar made to take it back. When Caesar withdrew, Vercingetorix pursued him with his army. This was a big mistake. The Romans defeated the Gauls and Vercingetorix had to escape with the remains of his army to a town called **Alesia**. He sent messengers to call upon all the tribes of Gaul to come to rescue him. They arrived in their thousands and the Romans found themselves with the enemy both in front and behind. However, after a savage battle the Romans won and Vercingetorix surrendered himself to Caesar. He was taken to Rome to be part of Caesar's triumph and, after some years in prison, he was executed.

Civil war

After ten years in Gaul, it was time for Caesar to return to Rome. While he had been away, things in Rome had gone from bad to worse. The triumvirate had broken up because Crassus had been killed, and Julia, Caesar's daughter and Pompey's wife, had also died. Lawlessness and fighting in Rome had caused the Senate to make Pompey consul on his own. He was afraid that Caesar was too popular.

Caesar marched south leading his legions until he reached the River **Rubicon**, the border between Gaul and Italy. Here the law demanded that he should give up his army and enter Italy as an ordinary citizen. If he did that, Caesar thought, he would be captured and killed by his enemy Pompey. According to the historian **Suetonius**, while he was making one of the most important decisions in his life, a man appeared, playing a tune on a pipe. The man waded across the river and some of his soldiers crossed the river to hear him play. Caesar took this as a sign: '*alea iacta est*,' he cried, 'The die is cast' ('die' is the singular of 'dice'), and he led his troops across the Rubicon. Today, if we make a decision which takes us past the point of no return we say that we have 'crossed the Rubicon'.

Pompey realised that his troops couldn't resist Caesar's and abandoned Rome. He sailed across to Greece with a large army. Caesar followed and in the **Battle of Pharsalus** (48 BC) he defeated Pompey who fled to Egypt. There he was murdered by order of the Pharaoh, who didn't want to upset Caesar.

The Ides of March

Caesar was now ruler of Rome. He was made Dictator for Life. Technically, Rome was still a republic, but the Senate and magistrates knew that they couldn't do anything without Caesar's approval. When Caesar had celebrated his triumph, he had worn a purple robe and sat on a golden throne, as was the custom. He carried on doing so and men who still believed in the Republic were afraid that he would soon become king, a word they hated and feared. Some of them plotted to kill him. On the Ides (15th) of March 44 BC, the day they chose, Rome was full of rumours, and Caesar's friends begged him to stay at home. Caesar's wife had had terrible nightmares and begged him not to go to the Senate. **Brutus**, who had been a close friend of Caesar but was now one of his enemies, pointed out that it would look very bad if the mighty Caesar stayed at home because his wife had had a bad dream. When Caesar entered, the Senators rose to their feet. The plotters gathered round him as if they wanted to ask him questions. Then, at a given signal, they drew their daggers and attacked him. Caesar saw Brutus among them. '*Et tu, Brute?*' he asked. ('You too, Brutus?') He then covered his head with

his toga while his attackers plunged knife after knife into his body. Strangely, the body of the mighty Caesar lay dead at the foot of the statue of Pompey.

How do we know?

Many historians have written about the wars between Rome and Carthage: **Appian**, **Polybius** and **Livy** are the best known. All the historians are either Roman or Greek and tell the story from the Roman side. We have nothing written from the Carthaginian point of view and we must always bear this in mind when we read stories of the Punic Wars.

As for Caesar's wars in Gaul, Caesar himself wrote a series of 'Commentaries' giving details of his campaigns and glorifying his triumphs. How trustworthy do you think these are?

Exercise 8.1

1. What were the inhabitants of Latium called?

2. Where in Greece was Pyrrhus the king?

3. How many cohorts were in a legion?

4. What was the *aquila* of a legion?

5. Which island was the cause of the war between the Romans and the Carthaginians?

6. Who was Hannibal's father?

7. In which year was the Battle of Cannae?

. . . .

Exercise 8.2

Complete the following sentences:

1. A century consisted of _____ men.

2. A legionary served for at least _____ years.

3. The Romans were ambushed in the Battle of Lake _____.

4. Fabius was called _____ because of his delaying tactics.

5. _____ cleared the Mediterranean of pirates.

6. _____ was the leader of the rebellious gladiators.

Exercise 8.3

Explain what is meant by the following:

1. a legion

2. a dictator

3. a 'pyrrhic victory'

4. *pilum*

5. a triumvirate

6. *auxiliaries*

Exercise 8.4

In 48 BC, Julius Caesar attacked a town called **Dyrrachium**. This is what he wrote about it:

A. 'Caesar's army, on the other hand, was in excellent health and had good supplies of water, as well as plenty of all kinds of food except corn. However, the weather was getting better every day and they were very confident as the corn ripened.'

Source: Caesar, De Bello Civile

Do you see how Caesar uses his own name? Another historian, **Plutarch**, writing his *Life of Caesar* more than one hundred years later, wrote the following:

B. 'At this time, too, it was said that some kind of an infectious disease was spreading through Caesar's army, a disease caused by the bad food they had to eat. And since Caesar was both short of money and short of food, it seemed likely that before long his army would break up of its own accord.'

Source: Plutarch, Caesar

Look carefully at sources A and B. Why do you think they say such different things?

. . . .

Exercise 8.5

1. Imagine that you are an elephant driver. Describe the journey with Hannibal across the Alps.

2. You are a gladiator, fighting with Spartacus against the Roman legions. Tell your story.

3. Describe the scene in the Senate as Caesar enters for the last time.

Chapter 9
Civil war

Mark Antony

Caesar lay dead at the foot of Pompey's statue, murdered by the men who wanted to restore the Republic. Brutus tried to make a speech to explain why the murder had been necessary, but the senators ran away, afraid that there would be more killing. Marcus Antonius, known to us as **Mark Antony**, had good reason to be afraid because he was

known to be a close friend of Caesar's. He hid while the murderers ran through the streets, telling the people that Caesar was dead and that the Republic had been restored.

Next day, in the forum, Brutus made a speech, telling the people to be happy because he had saved the Republic. The people began to mutter and then to shout insults. Eventually the crowd was so angry that Brutus and his companions hurried out of the forum and hid in the Capitol. Mark Antony now felt safe enough to go with his friends to the Senate. There it was agreed that Caesar should have a public funeral. Mark Antony asked permission to speak at the funeral, confident that he could persuade the people that Caesar's murder was a brutal crime. On the day of the funeral Brutus spoke first. He explained that he was Caesar's friend but that he loved Rome more. Caesar had been brave and for that he praised him, but he had also wanted to rule Rome on his own and for that he had killed him. By the end of his speech the crowd was on his side. Now Mark Antony rose to speak. He had come, he explained, not to praise Caesar but to give him a proper funeral. He went on to describe Caesar's qualities as a general, as a friend of the poor, as a personal friend. Even so, he said, Brutus, Cassius and the rest had their reasons for what they had done. He then paused, too overcome by tears, it seemed, to continue, and took the covering from Caesar's body.

When they saw the body with its twenty-three wounds, the crowd couldn't contain its anger. First they built a huge bonfire of household furniture, put Caesar's body on it and set fire to it; then they went in search of Brutus and Cassius and the others.

Octavian

Everyone now wanted Mark Antony to take control, but soon another man arrived in Rome. He was **Octavius**, the great-nephew of Julius Caesar, who had been chosen by Caesar as his heir. (When someone dies, the person he leaves all his possessions to is called his heir.) He now called himself Gaius Julius Caesar Octavianus and we call him **Octavian**. Soon the two men, together with a former supporter of Caesar's called **Lepidus**, formed a second triumvirate (42 BC) and each took a share of the Roman empire. Rome became a place of fear as enemies of the triumvirate were put to death in their thousands. Many senators fled to Greece where Brutus and Cassius had gone and where they had built up large armies. Mark Antony set off with a large army to Greece where he was soon joined by Octavian. They met the armies of Brutus and Cassius in the north of Greece at a place called **Philippi**. The **Battle of Philippi** (42 BC) was fought in two parts. In the first part, while Brutus fought against Octavian and managed to push

Octavian's army back and enter his camp, Cassius was defeated by Mark Antony. Cassius, after hearing a false report that Brutus had been beaten, killed himself. In the second part, Brutus led the remains of the Republican army into battle against Octavian and Mark Antony and was defeated. He too killed himself.

Cleopatra

Mark Anthony and Cleopatra

The triumvirate came to an end. Octavian thought Lepidus could not be trusted and ended their agreement. Two men now ruled the empire. Mark Antony went with his army to the East to put down rebellions, while Octavian returned to Rome. **Cleopatra**, the Queen of Egypt, had sent legions to help Cassius during the Civil War, so Mark Antony sent for her to ask her to explain her behaviour. When he saw her, however, it was love at first sight. Antony and Cleopatra spent the winter together. When Antony returned to Rome he married Octavian's sister, **Octavia**, to strengthen his friendship with Octavian. He took Octavia, a beautiful and intelligent woman, with him when he went to fight the **Parthians**. But she couldn't give him the son that he wanted, and when she gave birth to a second daughter he sent her home and sent for Cleopatra. In 32 BC he divorced Octavia and any remaining link between Antony and Octavian was broken. Civil war was now certain.

In 31 BC they clashed in a naval battle near Actium in Greece. Antony, supported by Cleopatra's fleet, advanced on **Agrippa**, Octavian's admiral, with two hundred and twenty warships. They were quinqueremes but, because of disease, they had too few sailors on board. Agrippa had smaller ships with better trained crews. His ships were also easier to move around. When she saw that the battle was going against Antony, Cleopatra and her fleet fled, and Antony was defeated. He managed to escape, but his legions saw who was going to win and deserted to the other side. Nineteen infantry legions and twelve thousand cavalry joined Octavian. Realising that it was all over, Mark Antony killed himself by falling on his own sword. Octavian was keen to keep Cleopatra alive and parade her in Rome as his prisoner. But, perhaps realising this, Cleopatra had an **asp**, a poisonous snake, smuggled into her room in a basket of figs. She picked up the snake and placed it on her arm. Within minutes she too was dead.

Augustus

Octavian insisted that the Republic would continue even though everyone knew that it was over. He refused to be Dictator (as Julius Caesar had been) but he used the power he had as a *proconsul* (we might say an 'ex-consul') in such a way that he had complete control of Rome and its provinces. He accepted the titles *Princeps*, which meant 'leading citizen', and *Augustus*, which meant 'worshipful'. Also, because he was in charge of the whole army, he was known as *Imperator*, which means 'General', but soon came to mean 'Emperor'. Augustus decided not to try to make the empire bigger but to keep what he had secure. He wanted peace for his people and, for only the third time in Roman history, the gates of the temple of Janus, which remained open while there was fighting in any part of the Roman world, were closed.

In 27 BC Augustus walked into the Senate and declared that he was going to retire. What a shock that was! All that the senators could imagine was a return to civil war. They begged him to think again and he changed his mind. Of course, he never really meant to retire. Years later, in 2 BC he accepted the title *Pater Patriae*, 'Father of his Country'.

Caesar's star

When Caesar was murdered, Octavian had seen to it that he was buried with almost royal honours. While the funeral was taking place, a comet had passed over Rome.

Comets were usually thought to be unlucky, but in this case it was suggested that it was the soul of Caesar going to join the gods. Julius Caesar was

deified (made into a god) and a star was placed over his statue. Coins were made with the faces of Julius Caesar and Augustus, father and son, with pictures of the *sidus Iulium*, 'the star of Julius'. Soon, other coins appeared with the face of Augustus and the words *divi filius*, 'son of the deified' or 'son of god'.

Coins:
Julius Caesar (left)
and Augustus (right)

Buildings

Augustus said: 'I found Rome a city of brick and I left her a city of marble.' To make Rome and the provinces more beautiful and to make clear to everyone the power of Rome, he rebuilt part of the forum with marble, both white and coloured, and repaired temples to encourage people to go back to the worship of their old gods. In the temple of **Apollo**, he put up a statue of himself as the god of music. He set up the *Ara Pacis*, the 'Altar of Peace', which had a carving of Augustus and his family and of other citizens with their wives and families, all shown looking happy with the peace which Augustus had brought.

Part of the Ara Pacis

The common feature of Roman building was the arch. One of the greatest problems a builder faces is how to support the weight of the walls and roof of a building. Using arches made buildings much stronger and the Romans could make buildings which were very big and pleasing to look at. They built the **Colosseum** in Rome, four storeys high and holding more than fifty thousand spectators; they built 500 kilometres of aqueduct to supply water for Rome; they built the **Pantheon**, a round temple which is still standing today; all these were made possible by using arches and columns. In their buildings the Romans copied the Greeks.

They used the Greek columns (see p.33) but, with their invention of cement and concrete and their use of baked brick, the Romans were able to make buildings the Greeks could never have imagined.

Aqueduct – the Pont du Gard in France

Literature

The age of Augustus is now considered the Golden Age of Roman literature. Writers of this time, encouraged and supported by rich friends of Augustus such as **Maecenas**, suggested the idea that, after years of bloodshed and civil war, Augustus was the saviour of the Roman people. Most famous of these writers was the poet **Virgil**. In Virgil's *Aeneid* (which you first heard about on p.52), Aeneas's son is called **Iulus**, the ancestor of Julius Caesar and, of course, of Augustus himself. At one point in his adventures, Aeneas has to go down into the underworld to find his father's ghost. There he sees a vision of all the great Romans who are to come, including Augustus, who will rule the world and bring a golden age of peace to Rome.

Horace (Quintus Horatius Flaccus) was another poet of this period. He wrote short poems (called odes) about his own life, his loves and private feelings. In many of these he praised Augustus. On the other hand, another poet called **Ovid** (Publius Ovidius Naso) angered Augustus by writing poems which didn't fit in with the ideas that the Emperor was trying to encourage. As a result, Ovid was sent away to live in misery, in a town on the Black Sea far from Rome.

How do we know?

As with Athens in the 5th century BC, Rome in the age of Augustus is well-known from the writing that has survived. The great writers of the age, Livy, Caesar, Cicero, Virgil, Horace, and Ovid are all well-known, especially to those studying Latin. Their works give us a very powerful view of Rome at the height of its power.

Inscriptions, too, are very useful in building up a picture of what life in Rome was like at this time. Here, for example, we have an inscription detailing what happened in 17 BC, when Augustus was leading a religious service:

'The next night, in a meadow by the Tiber, the Emperor Augustus sacrificed nine lambs and nine goats, to be offered to the Fates according to the Greek ritual… with the following prayer:

"O Moirae… I pray and ask you to strengthen the power of the citizens, the people of Rome, in war and peace… and look kindly on them, and on me, my family and household."'

Historians use all these various sources of information to build up the picture which we have of the Roman world.

Exercise 9.1

1. What are the names of the three men who formed the Second Triumvirate in 42 BC?

2. What are the names of the two leaders of the republican armies at the Battle of Philippi?

3. What was the name of Octavian's sister who married Mark Antony?

4. In which year was the Battle of Actium fought?

5. When could the gates of the temple of Janus be closed?

6. In which year did the Senate give Augustus the title *Pater Patriae*?

7. Name one of the rich friends of Augustus who supported writers?

8. In which year did Augustus die?

Exercise 9.2

Complete the following sentences:

1. Julius Caesar's body lay at the foot of the statue of _____.

2. Brutus and Cassius fought against Antony and Octavian in the Battle of _____.

3. Cleopatra sent legions to help _____ in the Civil War.

4. In 31 BC Octavian defeated Antony in the Battle of _____.

5. Octavian accepted the title _____, which means 'leading citizen'.

6. 'I found Rome a city of _____ and I left her a city of _____.'

7. According to Virgil, Augustus was descended from _____, son of Aeneas.

Exercise 9.3

Explain what is meant by the following:

1. *Pater Patriae*

2. a civil war

3. a quinquereme

4. *proconsul*

5. *Ara Pacis*

6. to deify

Exercise 9.4

1. Pretend you are Brutus, making your speech to the crowd at Julius Caesar's funeral. Say why the Republic is important and why Caesar's death was necessary.

2. Now pretend you are Antony. Mention all Julius Caesar's good points and say why he shouldn't have been murdered.

3. Describe the Battle of Actium from Mark Antony's point of view, mentioning the part played by Cleopatra.

Chapter 10
Roman entertainment

When you think of ancient Rome, you probably think of gladiators, chariot racing and Roman baths. Perhaps you have seen films such as *Spartacus*, *Ben Hur* or *Gladiator*, and know that the Romans were famous for their spectacular forms of entertainment. These spectacles developed out of what began as religious festivals. We have to remember that there were no weekends at that time and the only holidays people had were when there was a religious festival to celebrate. People were not allowed to work on holidays but nor did they have to go to the temple. They could either stay at home or they could go out in search of entertainment. Many families went to Rome because they had no jobs in the countryside, and large numbers of people who were unemployed and hungry could easily become dangerous, so the emperors used **panem et circenses**, 'bread and circuses', to keep the people happy. The bread was given to the poor and unemployed at a very low cost or even free; the circuses would take their minds off their problems.

The *Circus Maximus*

An artist's impression of the *Circus Maximus*

In Rome, chariot-racing took place in the *Circus Maximus*. Today, only the marble barrier (*spina*) in the middle of the track remains, but originally the *Circus* was six hundred metres long and could hold a crowd of two hundred and fifty thousand. Each chariot was pulled by four horses and started off in one of twelve starting-boxes (*carceres*). The race began when the starter dropped the *mappa*, a large white cloth. There were frequent crashes, and groups of slaves were used to cut the drivers free and to clear wreckages and bodies from the track. A driver belonged to one of four teams: Reds, Whites, Greens and Blues, with large groups of people supporting each team. The most successful drivers became as famous and popular as some footballers today.

The theatre

Ruins of the Roman theatre at Orange in France

Roman theatre began very much like Greek theatre. Early plays were performed in honour of a certain god, and most were Greek plays simply translated into Latin. Eventually Roman plays became more comic, usually rude, performances that could be enjoyed by most people. Most plays used similar types of characters that would be recognised by their costume, for example, a rich man wore purple, a poor man wore red, and a soldier wore a short cloak. The actors wore masks with exaggerated faces to show whether their characters were 'happy' or 'sad'. Women were not allowed on the stage, and so men played all the parts and used white masks for female characters.

Sometimes the writers of the plays received prizes if their play was popular, and groups of people were often paid to clap and cheer during some plays and to hiss and boo during others.

The amphitheatre

The largest **amphitheatre** in Rome was the *Colosseum*. It was circular in shape and the seating all round the arena could hold more than fifty thousand spectators. It was here that the gladiators fought. Gladiators were given special food and the best doctors. They were mostly slaves but sometimes freedmen signed on, hoping to become rich. Politicians who wanted to be popular, especially at election time, would pay for events at the amphitheatre, and the more gladiators they provided, the more popular they would be. At the end of a fight the winning gladiator, holding his sword to the throat of the man he had beaten, would look up to the politician, or the emperor if he was there, to ask whether he should finish him off or let him go. Often the loser would be allowed to live. Gladiators were valuable because it cost the trainer, the *lanista*, a great deal to train them. The life or death decision, which would often depend on how bravely the loser had fought, would be indicated by the thumb. Nobody is quite sure but it seems that the 'thumbs up', which to us means good news, was bad news for the gladiator.

An artist's impression of a *retiarius* fighting a *secutor* in the arena

There were several types of gladiator. There was the heavily-armed *secutor*, who had a helmet with only two holes to see out of. Then there was the *retiarius* who had no helmet and no armour but used a net, a trident and a dagger. Gladiators of the same type did not usually fight each other. The shows also included unusual wild animals fighting each other or being hunted, and criminals being executed, sometimes by being eaten by lions.

The baths

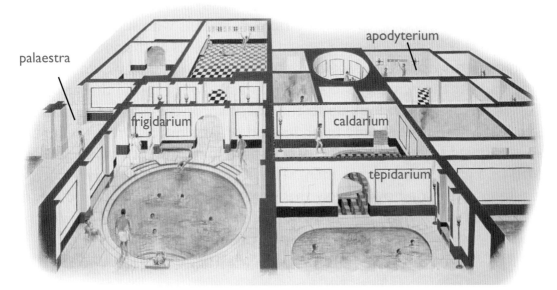

An artist's impression of the Roman baths in Bath, England

Most entertainments were saved for the holidays, but a visit to the *thermae*, 'the baths', was something most Romans enjoyed every day. They liked to make an early start and to get their jobs done before lunch. The afternoon could then be spent in the baths. The main reason they went to the baths was, of course, to get clean, but it was also a chance to meet friends and to take some exercise. Throughout the year Rome had lots of water from its aqueducts and at one time there were more than nine hundred public baths in Rome. Some were small and could hold about three hundred people, while others were enormous, with buildings as big as cathedrals which could deal with over a thousand visitors.

Usually a person would start in the *apodyterium*, the changing room, where they took off their clothing and left it with a slave. Then there was a massage with olive oil, games or wrestling in the *palaestra* or exercise yard, a dip in the warm water of the *tepidarium*, and a visit to the *caldarium*, the hot room. The heat of the *caldarium* would make the bather sweat. A slave would then scrape off the sweat and dirt with a *strigil*, a metal scraper. Last of all, the bather would go to the cold bath in the *frigidarium*. There was still plenty to do: gardens in which to walk; snacks and drinks to buy and athletics and wrestling to watch.

Tiberius and Caligula

When Augustus died in 14 AD his stepson **Tiberius** became emperor, taking on the family name of Caesar which he and all future emperors were to use. At first all went well, but as the years passed he began to believe that people were plotting against him. Executions became more common under Tiberius, and when his great-nephew **Caligula** took over in 37 AD things only got worse. Caligula was an especially cruel man who used his power to make other people suffer. Anyone who spoke out against him was sold into slavery, tortured or executed. It is not surprising that Caligula made plenty of enemies, and he was murdered in 41 AD. Tiberius and Caligula worried so much about things in Rome that the empire did not grow at all for thirty years.

Claudius and the conquest of Britain

Caligula's uncle **Claudius** came next. People around him thought, unfairly, that he was a weak fool. He had problems with his speech and movement, which made people think he was not good enough to be an emperor. However, his mind was sharp and he was able to command the empire better than anyone since the days of Augustus. In 43 AD, nearly a century after Julius Caesar, he led the Roman army back into Britain. Suetonius writes: 'He marched north through Gaul until reaching Boulogne; crossed the Channel without incident; and was back in Rome six months later. He had fought no battles and lost no men, but defeated a large part of the island.' When Claudius returned to Rome, he left commanders such as **Vespasian** to advance further into Britain. This continued under the next emperor, **Nero**, despite the efforts of brave British people, such as **Boudicca**, who tried to resist the Romans.

Nero

Nero was another cruel emperor who wanted to remove anyone who tried to resist him. For this reason he killed his mother, aunt and several other relatives. However, people still rebelled against him. In 66 AD the Jews in **Judaea** revolted when Roman soldiers failed to stop Greeks from looting a Jewish temple, or **synagogue**. The war which followed lasted seven years and ended with the destruction of the Temple of Jerusalem by the Romans. In 68 AD **Julius Vindex**, a Roman governor in Gaul, became the first of Nero's own men to rebel against him. **Sulpicius Galba** and **Salvius Otho**, two Roman commanders in Spain, helped him. Within a month Vindex was defeated and killed, but the Senate said Nero was a public enemy and sentenced him to death. Nero killed himself before he could be executed.

The year of the four emperors

The following year, 69 AD, has become known as the 'Year of the Four Emperors'. Nero's enemies fought among themselves to become emperor. **Galba** was first, and became unpopular for undoing the good things that Nero had done, and fining heavily any towns that did not accept him. The legions in Germany revolted, murdered Galba, and named **Vitellius** as the next emperor. On hearing the news, Galba's old friend **Otho** declared himself emperor. Unfortunately for him, Vitellius's supporters in the German legions were already marching south towards Rome. Otho tried to stop them but failed and, not wanting a civil war, he killed himself. Vitellius then had the same problem as Galba: the legions in Judaea and Syria named **Vespasian** as emperor. Vespasian's forces marched towards Rome. Vitellius was killed when the troops reached Rome and Vespasian became emperor.

The *Pax Romana*

Over the next fifty years the empire was peaceful with no serious uprisings. This period became known as a time of *Pax Romana*, or 'Roman Peace'. Between 112 and 116 AD, under the emperor **Trajan**, the empire grew eastwards into **Armenia** and **Persia**. This was the height of the empire: it stretched from Britain and Spain in the west to Egypt and Persia in the east, and the whole Mediterranean coastline was under Roman control.

From now on, the emperors concentrated on improving the empire they had rather than trying to make it bigger. For example **Hadrian**, instead of trying to take Scotland, built **Hadrian's Wall** across northern England to mark the border and to prevent tribes either side of it from joining against the Romans. The *Pax Romana*, however, was to end with the reign of **Commodus** (180-192 AD). Like Tiberius, he was convinced people were against him, and he and the emperors who followed had reigns marked by growing trouble and bloodshed.

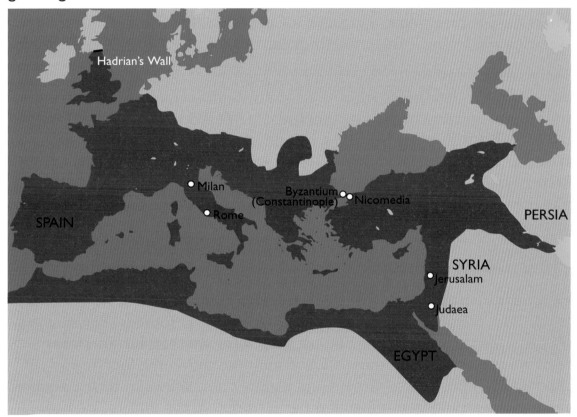

The Roman empire in the age of Trajan

The decline and fall of the empire

The Roman empire had one big problem which it never really solved: when an emperor died, who should take over? When a king dies his eldest son (or sometimes daughter) takes over, but after the emperor, who? Because there was no clear answer, many emperors were murdered. The emperor **Diocletian** realised that the empire was too big to be run by one man, so in 293 AD he divided the empire into two halves, East and West. There were to be two *Augusti*. One Augustus would rule the East from **Nicomedia**, a town near the Black Sea. The other Augustus would rule the West from **Milan** in Italy. Two deputies, called *Caesars*, would be appointed. They would rule over parts of the empire and take over when an Augustus died.

The emperor **Constantine**, who became Augustus of the West in 312 AD, put an end to this in 323 AD, when he took the whole empire under his command. He is famous for having made **Christianity** the religion of the empire. In 330 AD Constantine chose for his capital in the East a Greek city called **Byzantium**, which is at the entrance to the Black Sea, the very point where Europe meets Asia. He called it *Nova Roma*, 'New Rome', but soon everyone was calling it **Constantinople**.

The greatest threat to the Roman empire came from the invasions by tribes, from Germans (Goths, Ostrogoths, Visigoths, Vandals, Franks, Burgundians) and Huns, who came from Asia. Eventually, in 476 AD, the last emperor in the West, **Romulus Augustulus**, was driven out of Rome by German invaders. That was the end of the Roman empire in the West, but the Eastern Roman empire went on, with its capital in Byzantium, and Roman culture and traditions continued until 1453 AD, when Byzantium fell to the Turks.

How do we know?

Historians such as **Livy** and **Tacitus** give us a good picture of life in Rome at this time, but we also learn a great deal from other sources. For example, we learn about chariot racing not just from what we read, but also from what we see. A colourful mosaic found in Rome shows the four 'teams' of charioteers: Reds, Whites, Greens and Blues. It also shows us their costumes and equipment, and from this and other pictures we can understand how they rode. Some charioteers became famous, although they were slaves, and the most famous were pictured in mosaics such as these.

 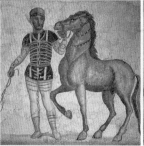  

A Roman mosaic showing the different teams of charioteers

In the same way, we know much about Roman theatre through paintings. This vase painting shows not only the actors in their masks and costumes, but also how the stage was set up and decorated. Notice the actors wearing their ugly, unreal masks. These would have helped the audience to recognise them more easily from far away.

We can also get a very good idea of what public buildings looked like because in some cases their remains still exist. Archaeologists have dug out the foundations of the *Circus Maximus* in Rome, which show the size and layout of the building, and allow us to build up a complete picture. With other buildings, such as the *Colosseum*, you can still pay a visit and walk through the original structure.

Exercise 10.1

1. How many people could sit in the *Circus Maximus*?

2. In the Circus what was the *mappa* and what was it for?

3. In the theatre what did a white mask mean about the actor?

4. At the Colosseum what three things did a *retiarius* use?

5. At the baths what was a *strigil* used for?

6. In which year was Caligula killed?

7. From where in Gaul, according to Suetonius, did Claudius set out across the English Channel?

8. Which emperor was responsible for the growth of the Roman Empire eastwards between 112 and 116 AD?

. . . .

Exercise 10.2

Complete the following sentences:

1. The emperors had a policy of *panem et circenses*, meaning _____ and _____.

2. In the middle of the track in the Circus was a marble barrier called the _____.

3. In chariot racing the colours of the four teams were _____, _____, _____ and _____.

4. At the baths the water in the *caldarium* was _____.

5. Tiberius was Caligula's great- _____.

6. Britain became part of the Roman empire when the emperor _____ sent an expedition there in 43 AD.

7. The 'Four emperors' of 69 AD were _____, _____, _____ and _____.

8. The empire in the West came to an end in _____ AD.

Exercise 10.3

Explain the following:

1. a *lanista*
2. the *apodyterium*
3. a *strigil*
4. *Pax Romana*
5. Augustus

Exercise 10.4

Look at the mosaics of the charioteers on p.102. These may have been four real charioteers, the stars of their day, or they may have been put in the mosaic simply to show the four teams. What are they holding, and what would they have used these things for? Why do you think their costumes appear to be padded? In what ways are they similar and different from today's jockeys in horse-racing?

Exercise 10.5

1. You are a Roman spending the day at the *Circus Maximus*. What do you do? Describe what you see.

2. How would you spend an afternoon at the Baths?

3. Describe a fight between a *secutor* and a *retiarius*.

4. Were the Romans who went to the amphitheatre any more cruel than modern people who go to a bull fight?

Greek history timeline

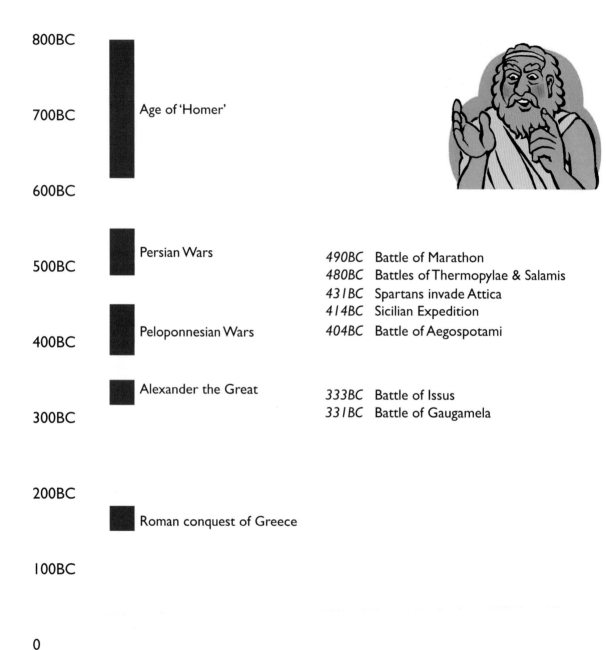

800BC

700BC — Age of 'Homer'

600BC

500BC — Persian Wars

490BC   Battle of Marathon
480BC   Battles of Thermopylae & Salamis
431BC   Spartans invade Attica
414BC   Sicilian Expedition
404BC   Battle of Aegospotami

400BC — Peloponnesian Wars

Alexander the Great

333BC   Battle of Issus
331BC   Battle of Gaugamela

300BC

200BC

Roman conquest of Greece

100BC

0

Roman history timeline

800BC	
	753BC Foundation of Rome
700BC	
Monarchy	
600BC	
	510BC Expulsion of Kings
500BC	
400BC	390BC Gauls capture of Rome
Republic	
300BC	280–275BC Pyrrhic War
	264–241BC 1st Punic War
	219–202BC 2nd Punic War
200BC	
	149–146BC 3rd Punic War
100BC	
0	27BC Augustus 1st Roman Emperor
100AD	98–117AD Roman empire at its height under Trajan
Empire	
200AD	
300AD	285–305AD Empire divided in two
400AD	
500AD	476AD End of the Western Empire

218BC Hannibal crosses the Alps
204BC Hannibal defeated at Xama

147BC Carthage destroyed

51BC Caesar's conquest of Gaul

31BC Battle of Actium

43AD Claudius's invasion of Britain

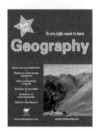

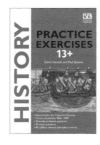

Galore Park

ISEB REVISION GUIDES

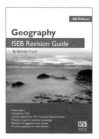

- All titles endorsed by the Independent Schools Examination Board

- Perfect for 11+, 13+ and scholarship entrance exam preparation

- Consolidates the key subject information into ONE resource making revision a breeze!

- Enables pupils to identify gaps in knowledge to focus their revision

- Worked examples show pupils how to gain the best possible marks

- Each guide includes practice material and answers to test understanding

Independent Schools
Examinations Board